PLAYING WITH
FIRE

KEVIN LEE
WITH DASHAWN TAYLOR

Playing With Fire

© 2017 by Kevin Lee c/o Next Level Publishing
All rights reserved.

No part of this book may be reproduced in any form, by any electronic or mechanical means (including photocopying, recording, or information storage and retrieval) without permission in writing from the author and publisher. Some names and identifying details have been changed to protect the privacy of individuals.

ISBN-13: 978-0-692-04620-3
ISBN-10: 0-692-04620-8

Makeup Artist: Sharon Richmond
Photographer: Bernadette Dare c/o Dare Digitals
Editing: Lorraine Elzia

WWW.NEXTLEVELPUBLISHING.COM

PLAYING WITH
FIRE

The road to success is not paved in gold, but in blood sweat and tears. So many of us have big dreams and never realize that the drive to reach our goals must be bigger than we can imagine. The incredible journey I have taken to reach my dream is one I would like to share with you. It is my hope that hearing my story can inspire others to take a chance and begin the journey to reach their own dreams. It won't be easy, but after all the struggles and sacrifices it will be worth it.

The struggles I have faced, and the sacrifices I have made, pale in comparison to the support I have received. Without such a wonderful network of family and friends I would have never made it to where I am today.

I would like to thank my amazing family for making this possible. My dad Henry Sr. was my first super hero and my mom Catherine was the driving inspiration for me to succeed. My stepdad, Mr. Sheldon, was amazingly supportive and I am forever grateful to him. May he rest in peace. My brother, Henry, bought me my first magic trick and was always there for me when I needed him the most. My sister Brigette, has always been a great big sister. She put in countless hours taking care of my daughter, Solina, while I traveled the world with my busy tour schedule. My sister Dawn, was my magician's assistant. She let me dress her up and saw her in half for my magic shows. A special thanks to my cousin Dennis who always played along with my fantasy of being in show business.

To my soulmate, the love of my life Patricia, I want to thank you for your amazing support and guidance along the way.

To my beautiful daughter, our journey together has been an amazing and touching story. I hope I made you proud being your father. This book is dedicated to you. Thank you for putting up with my crazy lifestyle.

Prologue

Most young kids from low-income families are given no more than a puncher's chance to make it out of the impoverished cities in America. For decades there has been a misleading stereotype that poor children only have a few options to be successful. Family, friends, teachers and even the media perpetuate this idea that poor children—especially minorities—can only elevate to the heights of real success by following in the footsteps of other people that look like them. Most kids are never taught how to truly think outside the box and blaze new trails to their ultimate goals.

I was never that type of child. I despised the thought of being like everyone else; I always knew I was different. There was always this feeling boiling in the pit of my stomach that reminded me that my life would be special. I clearly remember the first time this revelation became real for me. I was in my early teens and it all started with a sharp insult hurled in my direction.

"Kevin Lee! You will never amount to shit!!"

The hoarse voice of my science teacher echoed off the classroom walls. He towered over his desk and continued to berate me in front of the entire class. A thunderous round of laughter cascaded from all directions as my classmates took delight in my embarrassment. Just prior to the humiliating moment I was in my glory and doing what I did best at that age; I was being the class clown. I always joked around with the other kids, even in the middle of class. I was rarely interested in my school work, and frankly, I never took my education seriously. Even at a young age I could never wrap my mind around the importance of school. So while the teacher was trying his best to teach us about Isaac Newton, I was goofing off at my desk and stealing the spotlight, like a natural born entertainer.

But this day was different. My science teacher was fed up. His demeaning insult seemed to be directly aimed at my fragile self-esteem. He wanted to make me feel small, and for a brief moment he succeeded. The conviction in my teacher's voice almost convinced me that I would end up just like all the other deviants who never fulfilled their full potential.

If his ultimate goal was to crush my dreams and subdue my desire to be successful, my teacher failed miserably. The words that were meant to discourage me actually inspired and motivated me. From that day forward I vowed to prove him wrong. I was too young to realize the full power of the bitter man's words but I knew that there was no way I would end up as he predicted. A flame was ignited in my young mind and that message was burned into my memory. It fueled me on my journey to be great at anything I put my mind to. I wasn't sure how long it would take for me to become successful, but I always knew that something big would happen for me. Sometimes I look back on that day in science class and marvel at how a small spark of inspiration could explode into such a large flame that kept me driven. Despite the ill intentions of my teacher, I've remained grateful for his harsh words that set my conscious ablaze. He lit the fuse of motivation that was buried inside of me and I have been playing with fire ever since.

Chapter 1

The Genesis

To say I'm cut from a different cloth is an understatement. Who would have ever thought in their wildest dreams that a young, shy, black boy would grow up to be an internationally known magician and comedian? That just isn't a typical dream for most black boys; but then again, I was different from most black boys. Being a magician and a comedian was not only my dream for the future as a young boy; it became my livelihood as a man. I became a successful entertainer who has appeared on *HBO's Def Comedy Jam* and *NBC's Last Comic Standing*. I have traveled around the world several times, performed on top-of-the-line cruise ships, and even at some of the biggest colleges and universities in the country. Magic and comedy have afforded me the opportunity to be the opening act for the legendary Gladys Knight and to travel the world with some top celebrities like Sinbad, Wanda Sykes, Chris Tucker, Bernie Mac, and many others; the list goes on and on.

It's amazing how dreams are born. Mine was conceived innocently enough. A television commercial introduced me to what ultimately became my craft. I was thirteen years old when I saw this guy with well-manicured Caucasian hands doing these amazing card tricks across my TV screen. His sleight of hand movements had me mesmerized. The dexterity he showed in the TV advertisement for magic cards changed my life forever from that moment on. I couldn't get the image out of my head. The guy blew me away with those magic cards. I couldn't stop talking about the magician or the cards that I had seen advertised. The thought of being able to entertain and confuse people with my actions was very appealing to me. When my birthday came around I used some of my birthday money to get the cards. I'm sure my family thought it would be a passing hobby. I've always said that a $5 deck of magic cards has taken me around the world, and really it has.

It's an amazing thing that you can see someone on television, and then years later you're on television yourself, all because their moment on the small screen caught your eye. From the minute I was introduced to the magician on television, I wanted to be one myself. Once I got my hands on those cards I realized that magic was my destiny. As my life progressed, everything seemed exactly as I had envisioned when watching that advertisement and falling in love with the card tricks; but what came with it was something that was not shown on the screen. The image I saw on television that day didn't show all of the distractions, hardships, and ups and downs of this industry that I had to go through. That vision shown on the screen never let on to the fact that I would end up sleeping in the back of my cars, or that I would go hungry some nights, or even that I would be staying in rat and roach-infested hotels where hookers had just finished giving 'service' to their Johns. That initial vision from the television screen helped me to create some of the most amazing times in my life. It also helped to create some really bad times as well. But to see where I am now…it's just an amazing thing.

In sharing my experiences, I don't really know if this book will end up on the self-help section of the bookstore, but I'd tell anyone who's reading this book that I am a testament of believing in yourself and not giving up. If there were a way to search the phrase, *Never Give Up* in the dictionary, my face would be the illustration for that term. I am that guy who never gave up, no matter how hard things became.

There is an old saying that states: *Don't put all of your eggs in one basket*. Well, I can tell you right now, I did just that. Do I recommend it to people? Yes! Put all your eggs in one basket. That's my recommendation. Don't half step or play it safe. Life is about taking chances. It is the best way to go—nothing ventured, nothing gained. Anything worth doing should be done as if the only option available is succeeding. That's what worked for me.

During my career, if I had other options to fall back on, I probably would have quit a long time ago because it's been just that hard. But I really didn't have any other options. There was no Plan B for me. Basically, once I started along this career path, I didn't pick up any other trades as a young man. I had tunnel vision. All I saw was magic and comedy ahead of me. I didn't learn other things. I didn't want to. It was all about performing, magic, juggling, and teaching myself the craft. I was determined to be the best; a master in the craft of illusion and laughter.

I remember performing when I was fifteen years old. At the time I had gotten booked to perform at The Renaissance Festival. I saw this guy there who was eating fire. I asked him if he would teach me to do what he had just done, and he looked me up and down before saying, "No." I could tell from the way he addressed me that he had no interest in even talking to me, let alone showing me how to eat fire. I'm not sure if he felt insulted by my question or maybe even intimidated. It was clear he didn't want some young kid stepping into his territory. He failed in his attempt to deter me from learning something new and adding it into my act. I was anything but frightened or dissuaded by him. If anything, his conviction to keep it a secret only set a stronger desire within me to be able to do it myself. I eventually set my mind to it and taught myself how to eat fire.

That's how it's always been with me when it came to learning magic tricks. I've always possessed an insatiable desire to learn more about the craft. When I was younger I would go to the library and get books on magic. I spent countless hours studying and reading those books. I would practice the tricks from the books, and then I would go home and show what I had learned to my friends and family. They loved it. They didn't run away from me, or from what I was doing; they actually enjoyed my impromptu shows. My family was my first audience. They were the first to see all the new tricks that I would learn. Every time I tried a new trick on my family, it would drive them crazy. They had no clue how I was doing all the stuff that I was doing. Each time my family enjoyed one of my performances, it made me more excited to learn the next new trick.

I would learn something in a book, and then I would go to my mother's room and say, "Hey mom, look at this." She was always thrilled to see my latest trick. I remember when I first learned how to make a lit cigarette disappear. My mother was a smoker at the time and I thought she would get a kick out of watching me make one of her cigarettes disappear. Like a pro, my hands moved quickly. I lit the cigarette, and instantly it vanished into thin air. I watched her face for signs of excitement at me performing my new trick, but instead of excitement I saw nothing but fear. My mom couldn't figure out how the trick was done and she became afraid.

She said, "You're going to burn the house down! Tell me where that cigarette is."

She spent the whole evening worrying that I had thrown a lit cigarette somewhere in the room and that it was going to burn the house down later. Of course, that wasn't the case. It was a trick, but she still felt we were all in danger because she didn't know how the trick was done. I can still remember the look on her face. She was pretty freaked out about the vanishing lit cigarette trick. I was more concerned about her smoking in the first place, and now I'm just glad that she doesn't smoke anymore. It took a while, but she quit some years later. *Thank God.*

As you can imagine, being the only young boy in my neighborhood aspiring to be a magician made me stand out from the crowd. My friends thought I was crazy. I mean, here I was molding myself into Harry Houdini and Doug Henny while my friends wanted to be O.J. Simpson or Dr. J. Not me. I had different plans for my life. Doug Henny was one of the big-time magicians back in those days. He was the guy before David Copperfield; and of course, there was Houdini—the legend of magic. I always wanted to be like them. Those guys were my heroes, and honestly, they kept me grounded and focused on something positive. I didn't run the streets. It's sad to say, but most of my friends that I went to school with back then are now dead or in jail. The choices they made as teenagers caught up with them later in life. A lot of those guys ended up not becoming basketball stars nor football players, even though that's what everyone in my neighborhood wanted to be. They all would say, "I want to play in the NFL. I want to play basketball in the NBA." But not me; I was different. My dreams didn't involve a ball at all. I knew what I wanted, and that was to be Doug Henny; I wanted to do magic. Everybody thought I was crazy, but that dream…the dream of doing magic…kept my ass out of trouble. It kept me focused and it kept me in the house. It was just me and my books of magic. That was the only team I needed.

I remember watching the Jerry Lewis Telethon featuring the Rat Pack: Frank Sinatra, Sammy Davis Jr., and Dean Martin when I was thirteen years old. I would sit and watch those guys for hours at the time in amazement. I was completely blown away by them. They were so entertaining, funny, and talented. Everything about them was mesmerizing to me. I was like, *I want to be them when I grow up*. To this day, when you see me performing on stage, I'm wearing the Fedora like Sinatra used to wear, and the nice suits like Sammy, Dean, and Frank. Those guys were so cool. They were the true meaning of show business to me. They were full of charisma and they owned the stage. I became a big fan of all of their work; and to this day, even as a comedian and a magician, every time I step on stage, there's some Rat Pack coming out of my veins into the audience. I learned a lot from watching those guys. I still watch them on YouTube. They were unbelievable entertainers.

I could never be grateful enough for the direction in which my life turned after watching a simple sixty second commercial. From that moment when I got my hands on those magic cards, I knew that I had stumbled upon something special. I was never blessed with the opportunity to meet Frank, Sammy or Dean, but I can only imagine all the hard work and long hours that they endured to become legends.

I used their success as fuel to keep me going. Most people believe that the life of a great entertainer is full of leisure and fun times, but most people fail to see our immense hunger to be better. They don't experience the long hours, days and even years of sacrifice required to succeed. I never wanted to be just a good magician. I wanted to be *great*. I just needed to keep my nose to the ground and stay on the straight and narrow. As I set out on my journey, I learned that distractions, pitfalls and setbacks come in many forms. To reach my goals I had to find the unwavering strength that was buried deep inside of me.

Chapter 2

My First Love

*D**ead or in Jail*. If you were a black kid and growing up in the 60s and 70s, you were no stranger to the phrase; "Dead or in Jail." Parents, grandparents, teachers, aunts, uncles, scout masters, church leaders and even older siblings tried their best to drill that short but potent statement into the brains of the young kids they cared for. No one wanted to see their loved ones become incarcerated, or worse, leave this earth before their time like thousands of young black kids before them. My parents were no different. They loved me and my siblings very deeply. Having no love for their kids is something I could never accuse my parents of. Their love and support created a solid foundation that I utilized to pursue my dreams.

I spent part of my life growing up in Palmer Park, Maryland. I wouldn't classify my neighborhood as a war zone but it's a long way from Beverly Hills. Just like many of the middle-class areas in Maryland, we had our share of bad apples. And despite the fact that most of the kids in my neighborhood hung out at our house, my parents made sure that their kids did not become statistics. They always encouraged us to dream big and become successful. I'm sure my parents would have supported me in any endeavor I wished to pursue. They always stressed to me and my siblings that we could be anything that we put our minds to. And as fate would have it, I put my mind to magic.

"You know, most magic tricks are easy once you know the secret. With these magic cards it can be simple. You don't have to be a professional magician to perform these amazing card tricks because the deck works by itself."

The confident voice of Marshall Brodien echoed off the walls of my living room. I was just a young kid at the time but the television commercial grabbed my full attention. Marshall Brodien's hands moved with grace as he shuffled the deck of cards and performed a few amazing tricks that left me baffled. My eyes grew wide as saucers as I watched the wizard perform feats that seemed impossible in my young mind. I had never seen anything like it. The commercial was over in less than sixty seconds but the impact was eternal. Before I could even say the words out loud, my mind was already made up. I needed to have those cards.

As fate would have it, my birthday was coming up within a few weeks and I knew what I wanted. My mother and brother gave me a few dollars as a gift and that was all I needed. I headed down to the local drug store and searched for the magic deck that was permanently etched in my mind. I scanned the aisles like a hungry hawk searching for the package that I had seen on the commercial. And there it was. A simple yellow box that was worth only five dollars to People's Drug Store but that small box was worth the world to me. My face lit up like a Christmas tree when I made the purchase. I couldn't wait to get home and get started.

For the next few weeks I stayed inside the house and practiced on the deck of cards day and night. I read the instructions front-to-back multiple times and committed the illusions to memory. I tested my new found skills on my family and they loved it. The tricks were very challenging to me and I became lost in the thrill of learning more. I sought out any book that I could read in an effort to get better. Every day after school, I would come straight home, crack open my books and learn about the history of magic and the power of illusion. Sometimes I would stay up well after my bedtime just to learn as much as I could before I closed my eyes and dreamed about being a great magician. My love for learning was just as powerful as my love for magic. It became an obsession.

As I fell deeper into the world of magic, my loved ones were not the only people who noticed that I was changing. Before purchasing the TV Magic Cards, I was hanging out with a small group of kids from my neighborhood. We were typical boys growing up back then. We all wanted to be the popular kids in our school. We wanted to be the ones who ran in a pack, who joked around a lot and hung out at all the coolest places. My friends and I were heavily influenced by a movie called Cooley High. The kids in that movie talked cool, walked cool and dressed cool. And we wanted to be just like them. We bought clothes from the local thrift store and paraded around our neighborhood like we were being followed by a film crew. Every day, after school, we would hang out and play the role of a cool group of kids.

But that all changed once I got my hands on the magic cards. I slowly drifted away from my friends and traded in my khakis and baseball jackets for magic cards and books about Harry Houdini. None of my friends developed an interest in the world of magic like I did. I didn't mind going at my new-found hobby alone. I always considered myself a leader and I was no stranger to trying something new without the approval of my peers. I found myself in the library every week searching for new books about great illusionists and magicians from various eras. Stories about Harry Blackstone, Dai Vernon and Alexander Herrmann filled my thirst for knowledge. Success stories about Siegfried and Roy, Doug Henning and Mark Wilson inspired me to study long and hard until I was great. I grabbed book after book and took them home to study. Some of the stories were so intriguing that I refused to return them to the library. I treated my bedroom like a study hall where I learned something valuable with each passing day. The knowledge I gained from those books helped me prepare myself for the long journey that was ahead of me.

One day while I was looking at the large stack of books that I had accumulated over the long months of studying, an alarming thought came to my mind. I had studied dozens of great magicians, both past and present, and there was something missing. Or should I say *someone* missing. Of all the great stories and historic records, I had not come across one person that looked like me. I was only a teenager at the time but I was self-aware and conscious of the fact that I was a black boy in America. I refused to believe that there were no magicians of African descent anywhere on the planet. I found myself searching through the library to find a book, any book that told the story of a black magician. There were none available. Even at a young age, the thought didn't sit well with me.

Despite my disappointment I did not give up on my ambition to be a great magician. It was hard for me to understand why I was unable to find someone that looked like me who mastered the art of illusion. Instead of allowing my disappointment to hold me back, I decided to use it as fuel. I read more books and practiced long hours into the night to learn every trick I could. I was only thirteen at the time, but I took my magic very serious. I'm sure my family thought I had lost my mind. They were constantly being forced to sit through long hours of practice-runs and unrehearsed bits. But through it all my family remained supportive.

A few months after I purchased my first deck of magic cards, I learned a valuable lesson about show business. After months of reading, studying and practicing, I was finally ready to show off some of my skills to a larger audience. I got my first opportunity during our family reunion that following summer.

My grandmother Dorothy knew that I was very excited about my new love for the art. She always got a kick out of watching me perform my magic tricks. She wanted everyone to know about my talent so she asked my entire family to come downstairs into the basement. My grandmother set up a few chairs and made sure everyone had a good seat to watch her grandson perform. It was my first time doing magic for a full audience so I asked my younger cousin Dennis to be my first magician's assistant. Dennis always looked up to me so he agreed to help me out.

I started the show with a few card tricks from my magic deck. I was also studying a lot about sleight of hand tricks so I decided to show my family what I had learned. They loved it. It felt good to dazzle my family and keep them guessing about how the tricks worked. With every successful illusion I gained more confidence. After the show was over my family even clapped for me as if I was a world class entertainer. I couldn't thank my grandmother enough for helping me perform my first show. I could tell that she was proud of me, but my grandmother had another surprise.

As everyone in the basement clapped for my homemade show, my grandmother passed around a hat. She told everyone to show their support for my magic. "This show is not free," my grandmother said. "We have to pay these boys."

To my surprise, my grandmother was able to raise close to fifty dollars for both my cousin and me. During my long hours of shuffling cards and practicing magic tricks, it never occurred to me that I could get paid to be a performer. I was so intrigued by the mastery of the tricks that I never thought about making money or turning my talent into a career. From that day, I started to become interested in the business of entertainment. I learned a valuable lesson in the basement that summer day. My grandmother planted a very important seed in my mind. The idea of earning money and becoming a successful magician seemed like an exciting idea to me. In addition to studying the art of illusion I decided to study long and hard about the business and learn how to earn money.

By the end of the summer I was well on my way to taking my magic seriously. I had visited the thrift store on a number of occasions and purchased an outfit that I would use in my shows. I bought a flashy suit, white gloves and even a top hat. I wanted to emulate all the great magicians that I read about. I purchased more magic kits and any other books I could get my hands on. Every day after school I would hop on my bike and ride around with my younger cousin Dennis. We would do magic for anyone that would watch us. We were both young and naïve but that didn't stop us from drawing a crowd; or even stealing someone else's crowd.

One day while we were riding around on our bikes we noticed a large crowd gathering at the local McDonald's. A man dressed as the world-famous Ronald McDonald clown was performing magic for a group of people in the restaurant parking lot. He entertained the young kids with his tricks and the audience loved him. My cousin and I didn't think twice about what we had to do next. We quickly set up behind the crowd and started doing magic tricks of our own. A few onlookers took notice and before long our audience started to grow larger. Before our show was over we were able to draw just as much attention as the main attraction. My cousin Dennis and I didn't try to steal the spotlight to be rude. I was still a young magician and I was hungry for the challenge of entertaining a crowd.

It felt good to expand my act. Impressing my family was one thing, but engaging a group of strangers was a different ball game. I knew I had to get better if I wanted to become a famous magician. As my confidence grew, so did my act. Every week I was thinking of new places to set up and test out my skills. I even went back to the library where I "*borrowed*" all those books from. I asked the manager if I could perform a show there.

"You want to perform a magic show here in the library?" The Librarian asked as she glanced down at me.

"Yes." I eagerly responded.

"How much do we have to pay you?" The Librarian asked.

The question stumped me for a moment. I had never charged anyone for my magic and I was unaware of the going rate for a magician. I decided to say the first number that came to my head.

"Uhhhh….a hundred bucks." I nervously responded.

"Deal." The manager nodded without hesitation.

With a handshake and a smile I officially became a working magician. The library agreed to make a flyer for me and help me promote my first show. I just needed to add one last piece to my act—a stage name.

I idolized two people when I was a young boy—the legendary martial artist Bruce Lee and the great escape artist Harry Houdini. Both men had a resounding effect on me and both men inspired me to be great at anything I put my mind to. Reading about these men and studying their lives constantly encouraged me. I wanted to show my gratitude for their amazing careers. So when it was time for me to choose a stage name I decided to pay homage to my idols. A few weeks later I found myself back in the library. But this time I was not there to study any books. I was there to perform my act. The manager was able to drum up a nice sized crowd for me and I was surprised by the turnout. Despite my nervousness, I was able to put on an excellent show. The audience loved the tricks and my sleight of hand illusions. I tried out a few new ideas and grew more confident with each successful turn. It felt good to please the crowd. There I was in the middle of a place where hundreds of stories were told about great magicians and illusionists and I was starting the first chapter of my story. It was an amazing accomplishment. After my show I received a large round of applause. And from that day, *LeeDini The Magician* was born.

Chapter 3

The Color of Magic

While most kids my age were doing odd jobs and humping paper routes to make money, I was literally working my magic throughout the DMV area. I had managed to turn my favorite hobby into a budding career. Every week I found new and creative ways to make money from my magic. Getting paid to do something that I loved only energized me to grow as an artist and entertainer. My cousin Dennis and I continued to ride around on our bikes and perform in front of any crowd we could find.

As I approached my fourteenth birthday, I started putting advertisements in the newspaper. I also passed out business cards to promote my new act as LeeDini the Magician. Before long, my business started booming. People would call the house all the time for me. It was surprising how successful my ads were. Every weekend I was getting booked to do birthday parties and family functions throughout the area. I would also get a lot of work based on word-of-mouth. Parents would see my show and recommend me to their friends. I was always grateful for the new business.

With every paid event, I wanted to make my act bigger and better. I purchased a few birds and even bought a rabbit to add to my set. Even at such a young age, I understood the concept of keeping my act fresh and new. I learned more sleight-of-hand tricks and began to make my illusions more elaborate. The tricks became harder to learn and I spent long hours perfecting them. If I wasn't practicing in my backyard, I was locked in my bedroom with my books and my magic kits. No matter how many tricks I learned, I always had a hunger to learn more. I wanted to make a good impression on all of my audiences and I wanted them to remember me.

On a typical weekend, I would make anywhere from two hundred to three hundred dollars. That was very good money for a young teenager with no bills. I performed for large and small audiences alike. Some customers would request me for a family gathering with twenty people and some would request me for over fifty people. Some of the houses I visited were simply awe inspiring. I didn't have a driver's license back then so my stepfather Mr. Sheldon would drive me to most of the locations. He was also impressed with the luxury structures that sat in the middle of these affluent neighborhoods. Week after week I would perform for dozens of families from various ethnic backgrounds. It was hard not to notice the stark difference between me and my audience. I was never uncomfortable performing for people of other races but I began to wonder why I never got booked by any African American families. I felt like I was back in the library searching for people that looked like me. Once again, I refused to allow my disappointment to get the best of me. I didn't need validation for my passion. But my curious mind wrestled with a peculiar question. *Is it possible that I was the only black boy that enjoyed magic?*

Because my young career was clearly flourishing, I decided to leave that question for another day. There was so much for me to learn and so little time. I was studying magic so much that my school work suffered as well. I didn't mind the fact that my grades were slipping. Who needed school work when I had already made up my mind that I was going to be a world-famous magician? When it was time for me to find more information on the world of magic I turned to Al's Magic Shop in Washington, D.C. The shop was located in the northwest section of the city. I had discovered the location after researching different stores and shops to find books. When I walked into Al's it felt like I was entering another world.

The shop was owned by an older gentleman named Al Cohen. He ran the shop with his sons and a few other employees. The shop was a gold mine of information. Al Cohen had hundreds of books and magazines on the subject of magic. There were rows of magic kits, tricks and games that I had never seen before. I felt like a toddler in a candy factory. After visiting the shop just one time I immediately discovered that magic was not only an exciting pastime, it was an enormous industry. I started learning of magicians that I had not read about in the library. Dozens of artists had their own card decks and booklets to help anyone that was willing to learn. I couldn't get enough of the store.

I decided that I would make Al's Magic Shop my second home. If I was not booked to do an event I would head down to the shop every weekend. The shop would open at 8:00am and I would be on the first train to D.C. I would stay there for hours and hours and study as much as I could. The shop kept me out of trouble and helped me to stay away from many situations that could ruin the life of a typical teenager.

Dozens of young magicians and famous entertainers visited the shop every week. I tried to meet them all. I wanted to be a part of the excitement of the business so I asked a lot of questions and learned as much as I could. After several long days and afternoons in the shop, a nagging realization returned to my mind. I was the only black boy in the shop most of the time. When those young magicians came to see Al and his family I noticed that none of them were black. Of all the parents that purchased magic decks and kits for their kids, none of them were black. Not even the tourists that just visited the shop were black. Again, I was left with a perplexing reality that it was possible that I was the only black kid that enjoyed magic.

One day while I was in the shop I scanned the back wall that Al had created with pictures of all the famous people that came to his establishment. Al was clearly a heavy hitter in the industry and a lot of celebrities visited him when they were in town. I recognized a lot of the famous faces but one in particular caught my attention. Near the top of the wall for everyone to see was a photograph of Muhammad Ali. There was a signature from the boxing legend that was made out directly to Al. Anyone that had a pulse back then was a fan of the Greatest of All Time and I was no different.

I asked Al about the photo. "Wow, you know Muhammad Ali?"

"Oh yes, Ali comes in here all the time." Al responded. "Whenever he is in the D.C. area he comes in and buys magic tricks."

"So Muhammad Ali does magic tricks, too?" I asked.

"Ali loves magic." Al laughed. "He does card tricks all the time and he's good."

I was speechless. For months I was searching for anyone in the world of magic that looked like me. Never in a thousand years would I have guessed that the greatest boxer to ever live was also a magician. I felt proud to learn the news. It helped me get over any brief moment of doubt that I was heading in the right direction. Knowing that I was studying in the same magic shop as Muhammad Ali made me want to work that much harder.

From that day forward I wanted to challenge myself more. I wanted to expand my act even further beyond just card tricks and small illusions. I started buying more elaborate kits and studying harder levels. It was grueling research and long hours of studying. But I wanted to be like those great magicians with their polished acts. I wanted to learn from the best. In addition to learning from these great artists in the books and magazines, I also learned a lot from watching their live shows.

My stepfather Mr. Sheldon was very instrumental in my success during the start of my young career. In addition to making sure that I traveled safe to all of my paid gigs, my stepfather also did anything he could to keep me inspired. One day he surprised me with tickets to see a live magic show starring Harry Blackstone. In all of my research I had never come across the name Harry Blackstone so I assumed he was a local act. Once we arrived at the large theater in northern Virginia I quickly realized that this man was no small-time talent. From the moment he appeared on stage, Harry Blackstone totally blew me away.

"Magic is the great theater of imagination. The pondering of the what if. In magic, if you believe in something strong enough a great magician can make it a reality."

Harry's voice commanded the attention of the entire audience.

He began his show with large illusions and eye popping effects. The production was amazing. As I sat there in awe of his work I couldn't help but notice that he was actually a very funny entertainer. His large tricks and grand illusions were breathtaking. But it was the small bits and hilarious jokes that made him stand out from anyone that I had seen before. In the middle of his set he would invite people up onto the stage and perform small gags and jokes that kept the audience rolling. It was very entertaining.

Before watching Harry Blackstone, I had never realized that I could be funny as a magician. I didn't have to dress up like Clark Gabel every day and become a serious character with no personality. The jokes added another level to the show. It kept the audience begging for more. I decided from that day that I would refine my act. I credit Mr. Blackstone for planting that seed from afar. Adding the comedy was one of the best decisions I ever made for my career. I was naturally a funny person, so the transition to a magician-comedian was a lot of fun. In the beginning it was challenging to write jokes that would accompany the magic tricks. But I quickly got the hang of it and the jokes helped the flow of my developing act.

A few weeks after witnessing the amazing show of Harry Blackstone, my stepfather suggested that I sign up at a magic school. Naturally I agreed and started taking classes at the Dream Wizards Magic Shop. The classes were taught by a professional magician from the area. He was a really nice guy and very good at his craft. I was also excited to see that he was an African American. It was good to know that Muhammad Ali and I were not the only black magicians on the planet.

During the classes at Dream Wizards I learned more advanced methods of producing magic shows. The lessons were challenging and I was inspired to add additional tricks into my act. We were instructed to read from a book written by a great magician named Tony Slydini. He was originally from Italy but he made an incredible name for himself in the United States. His sleight-of-hand tricks were downright miraculous. He had mastered scores of techniques and various degrees of misdirection. The secrets he divulged in his books were invaluable. They were designed to help any passionate young magician learn from his experience. And I was surely filled with that passion.

The magicians and the illusionists that I studied when I was a young boy helped to fuel my love for magic. There was no such thing as a trivial lesson that I learned from any one of them. Every book I read had a lasting effect on me and every tip was priceless. There are not enough words in the English dictionary to describe the feeling of learning a new trick and having the ability to execute it flawlessly. From the age of thirteen I have been utilizing the knowledge that I gained over the years. Every part of my act was built using the bricks of wisdom that were passed on to me through reading, studying and watching the legends. I owe a great deal of my success to their legacies.

It was once said that every successful person has a painful story. I am no exception to that rule. My journey has endured many obstacles. My road is littered with disappointments. I have been able to put some of the unfortunate experiences behind me. Other experiences will stay with me for the rest of my days. The scars that are too deep to heal still linger. And those growing pains are unforgettable. I learned at an early age that you must be strong as steel to follow your dreams. And there is no such thing as an easy path. Sometimes life will deal you the ugliest cards and there is no magic trick that can make them disappear.

Chapter 4

We Are Family

Before discovering my love for magic, I was like any other young boy growing up in a large family. I played a lot and enjoyed goofing around with my siblings. We were all very close as kids. My parents made sure of that. They taught us to always love and respect each other. Even during the time when we lived in separate homes, we were still a loving family.

My parents were high school sweethearts. They were both raised in Chapel Oaks, Maryland. Their relationship began like a Hollywood love story. My father was a star player on the high school football team and my mother was a stunning cheerleader. Their teenage romance evolved into a special bond and they eventually married. My older sister Brigette was their first child. She was followed by my older brother Henry. By the time I was conceived my parents' relationship was already on the rocks. My family always joked that I barely made it into this world. I was the product of their last effort to reconcile. Unfortunately, their union eventually ended and my parents divorced when I was just a toddler.

Being separated from my dad was tough for me when I was younger. For as long as I could remember I always looked up to my father like he was a superhero. He was a truck driver back then. It seemed like he stayed on the road all the time. My father would drive his eighteen-wheeler across the country. One of my earliest memories of my dad was watching him emerge from that monster of a machine. It seemed to be as big as a house. I couldn't believe that my father knew how to drive that thing. One day he let me sit on his lap and grab the steering wheel inside of the big rig. I was simply amazed by my dad. I was convinced that he had to be the strongest man on the planet to handle such a magnificent truck.

Just like all superheroes my father would pop up from time to time. As a young boy I didn't see much of him. He would pick me up on the weekends and take me to visit family. Sometimes I would visit my grandmother Ruth's house in Chapel Oaks, Maryland and sometimes I would visit my grandmother Gertrude's house in Arlington, Virginia. It was never my father's intention to stay with us. He had his own life. My dad would drop us off at a relative's house and soon after he would disappear again. Eventually I got used to the routine. I could never tell how long he would stay away but it was always good to see him once he returned.

Not long after my parents divorced, my mother began to struggle financially. After a while, all her kids ended up living in separate homes. My sister Brigette stayed with my grandmother Dorothys' Godmother Amanda in D.C. while my brother Henry stayed at my grandfather Henry Sr's and Grandmother Gertrude's house in Arlington, Virginia. I ended up staying with my mother's Aunt Cecelia in Chapel Oaks, Maryland. My mother married her second husband, Earl Brooks, and they added another blessing to our family. Her name was Dawn. Although she was not my father's daughter we never considered Dawn to be our half-sibling—she was our sister.

Dawn was the only child, at that time, who stayed with my mother. She was much younger than the rest of us. I was around six years old at that point and it was no fun being separated from my brother and sisters. I played with my cousins a lot but it was nothing like playing with my siblings. Brigette, Henry and I lived in different cities for several years. I would see them at family gatherings from time to time but not nearly as much as I wanted to be around them. I was estranged from my siblings so much back then that it was difficult for me to recognize them sometimes.

One day my mother picked me up from my Aunt Cecelia's house in Chapel Oaks, Maryland. She told me that she was taking me to a birthday party at my Aunt Gertrude's house. As always I was excited to be around my family so I couldn't wait to get to the party. I remember riding by the National Zoo as my mother made her way to a very large house located on the Northwest side of Washington, D.C. The old-fashioned house reminded me of something out of a Dracula movie. I stayed close to my mother as we made our way through the house and into the basement. I remember smelling a distinct odor of mildew and moldy water as we walked down the creaky stairs.

The dusty basement was filled with kids. I recognized a few cousins and other family members but there was one face that stood out to me. In the middle of the dreary cellar was a pretty young girl who seemed to light up the room. She was sitting behind an old piano. The girl was tall and fair skinned and I could tell that she was older than me. Her hair was split down the middle with two jet black pony tails on each side. She was playing the keys on the piano and singing the song *"Lean on Me"* by Bill Withers.

"Wow, that is a pretty girl." I mumbled under my breath. I turned to my mother and asked her the question that was burning in my mind. "Who is that?" I uttered as I pointed to the young girl behind the piano.

"That's your sister, Brigette." My mother quickly responded.

The answer shocked me. I had met my older sister a few times but I was too young to remember. She was so talented and I couldn't help but be very impressed by her. I didn't see a lot of Brigette in those early years but after meeting her again at the birthday party, I was proud to call her my big sister.

My brother Henry was a different story. I had seen a lot more of him as a little boy. On most weekends, my father would pick me up from my Aunt Cecelia's house and take me to spend a few days with Henry at my grandfather's house. His name was Henry Lee, Sr. He was my father's father. My grandfather lived in Arlington, Virginia with his second wife Gertrude. Those days and weeks that we spent in Arlington were some of the best days of my early childhood. I was able to play with a lot more kids that were my age, and hanging out with my brother made those days so much more enjoyable. Like many kids growing up back then, my brother and I would get into a lot of trouble together. I remember hanging tight with him as we played all types of sports. Baseball, football, basketball; you name it. Henry and I would try our hand at anything to have fun. When there were no sports to play, we would hang out in the woods and explore the creeks in the area. We both were very adventurous boys growing up.

If we were not in Arlington, Virginia together, my dad would drop us off at our grandmother Ruth's house in Chapel Oaks, Maryland. She was my dad's mother. My grandmother Ruth had remarried after her divorce with Henry, Sr. and was now married to my grandfather Mac. Because my grandfather was a farmer, my grandparents had converted their land into a small farm. It was on that farm where my brother Henry and I got into the most trouble. We loved that farm. It was so much mischief to explore. Every day my brother and I would find new ways to drive my grandfather Mac crazy. If we were not climbing on the roof of the chicken house, we were climbing the trees and eating the fruit in the backyard. Sometimes we would even get lost in the woods behind the house and find more trouble to get into. It became a daily goal to make our granddaddy Mac yell at us.

The worse part about those weekends with my brother was going back to my Aunt Cecelia's house alone. For a long time, we would become separated after a fun-filled weekend and those breaks in between were not easy. The routine of seeing my brother and sister sporadically went on for some time. I was not the only one that grew tired of the Lee children being separated from each other. As fate would have it, all of that changed.

One afternoon, when I was about seven years old, I was in the front yard of my Aunt Cecelia's house. I was playing alone when suddenly I felt a heavy hand snatch me from behind. Before I could make a sound, I was being carried away like a heavy suitcase and tossed in the backseat of a car. I didn't know what to think. My young mind couldn't process what was going on. I had heard about kids being kidnapped but I never thought it could happen to me. The heavy doors slammed shut and the car sped off down the road. I looked around with a confused look on my face. After a few minutes, I realized something was different. My sister Brigette and my brother Henry were in the back seat with me. It appeared that my siblings had been snatched too. I looked to the front seat and got a good look at my kidnappers. It was my mother and my stepdad Earl Brooks.

After years of the Lee children living with various family members, my mother was finally ready to get her kids back. I was too young to understand the full story but some of my mother's relatives were unwilling to relinquish her children without a fight. My mother decided to take matters into her own hands. She wanted to make my family whole again, and having my sisters and my brother under one roof was something that I always wanted. For the first time, we were all together—finally.

Despite the drastic measures my mother had taken to get her children back, she did not move us very far from my Aunt Cecelia's house. In fact, our new home was in the same neighborhood in Chapel Oaks, Maryland. When we arrived, I noticed that my mother and Earl had already moved most of our stuff into the new house. We didn't have a lot of furniture but my mother made the best of her new home. We were still struggling financially back then. But as kids, we were too young to notice. We were in our own world and excited to be around each other again. Besides, who needed money when you had three talented kids in the house that could turn any typical day into a full-blown concert.

Oh baby, give me one more chance...To show you that I love you...Won't you please let me back in your heart...Oh darlin', I was blind to let you go...Let you go, baby...But now ...since I've seen you... it is on...

Our stereo blasted the hit song *"I Want You Back"* by the Jackson 5. My sister Brigette and my brother Henry held broomsticks in their hands and sung along with the music. Having little furniture in our bedroom made it easier to transform our space into a make-believe dance floor. My sister would always pretend to be Jermaine Jackson and we always made Henry play Tito Jackson. He hated playing Tito.

I was always in the front playing Michael Jackson. I was the most talented one of the siblings and I always could sing and dance. I had no clue at the time that I would be performing nightly for audiences across the world. But even back then I had a knack for entertaining people. My sister Dawn was too young to play with us at the time so Brigette, Henry and I would always pretend to be the Jackson 5 or The Sylvers. We were all good singers and dancers. We thought we would be a famous group one day.

If we were not dancing and entertaining each other, my siblings and I would find other ways to have fun. My mother did not have a lot of money to buy toys for us so we figured out ways to make our own toys. When we wanted to play basketball, my brother and I would cut out a laundry basket and nail it to a tree. We didn't have a real basketball court back then but we were happy with what we had. When it was time to go bike riding, my brother and I would find ways to build our own bicycles and go-carts. Sometimes we would steal a shopping cart from the local supermarket. We would take off the wheels and nail them to a sturdy piece of plywood. Once we added a long stick to the front, we would have a homemade scooter to play with. If we wanted bikes, we would find old parts around the neighborhood and put them together. We would clean the rusty body frames and add tires to them. If we couldn't find good tires on the street we would steal inner tubes from the local hardware store and put them inside the tires. Our bikes never looked like the nice ones in the newspaper advertisements, but they worked just as well. For Henry and I, making our toys was just as much fun as playing with them.

As me and my brother Henry grew tighter as siblings, my sister Brigette and I had a typical brother-sister relationship. When we were younger we would all play together outside and find things to get into. Sometimes we would go down to the creek and catch tadpoles to bring home. Other times we would make up games to keep us all entertained. As Brigette became older she played less with her younger brothers. She was our big sister and she became a teenager before us. Brigette started to get into her own things and her new friends were maturing well beyond exploring the woods and playing with homemade toys. Brigette and all her friends referred to me as their *little* brother.

Although Brigette and I loved each other very much we would get into a lot of fights when we were younger. With me being the youngest boy, Brigette and I would clash occasionally about trivial things. Most incidents would escalate into loud arguments and sometimes even fist fights. Brigette was much bigger and stronger than me so I would lose most of those fights. I remember Brigette even blackened my eye during one of those confrontations. To this day we laugh about all the squabbles we had as kids.

No matter how many arguments and fights we had as children, we were still family. No amount of words, punches or tears could separate me from my sister Brigette. We never let any of our disagreements fester too long. Our sibling love was iron-tight and it has remained strong to this very day. Those early days with Dawn, Henry and Brigette were priceless to me. After being separated from my siblings for many years, it was a blessing to have them in my life full-time. Our family may have been poor financially but we were rich with love. Some people take their families for granted. But that wasn't the case with us. We were always tight. But like all families, there were a few relatives around us with malice in their hearts. They posed as family but they were really demons in disguise. Nothing in my young life could have prepared me to face those monsters. I suffered an attack on my innocence and it would take a miracle for me to survive it.

Chapter 5

Family Pain

Pain and disappointment is an unavoidable part of the human experience. We all can remember the darkest days of our lives and some people are even defined by them. Those who are able to escape their childhood unscathed are considered the lucky ones. But for some of us, the emotional scars that we receive at an early age are too deep to ignore.

As a child, growing up in a large family gave me a sense of security. But there were also times when I felt confused. It was hard for me to understand how the protectors in my life could suddenly transform into the monsters in my life. My young mind couldn't process how some of my relatives could unleash such deep physical and emotional punishment on me. I was barely eight-years old when I learned a painful life lesson. Even before I discovered the power of magic and illusion, I learned that people could hide their malicious intentions behind something as simple as a familiar face. I never had any doubt that my family loved me. As I got shuffled from one house to another I always felt that my family cared for me and would never do anything to hurt me. However, there were some relatives that were not so kind to me. Of all the houses I lived in when I was younger, staying with my Aunt Cecelia proved to be some of the toughest days of my early childhood.

In the summer of 1965, then President Lyndon B. Johnson sent thousands of soldiers to enter a conflict known today as the Vietnam War. The horrific confrontation in Southeast Asia lasted for nearly ten years and cost over 50,000 U.S. soldiers their lives. Like all major conflicts, the war changed the world and affected millions of families back in the United States. Vietnam veterans throughout the nation found it difficult to readjust to a normal life after the traumatizing experience of surviving the war. My Uncle Paul was one of those survivors.

Soon after returning to Maryland from active duty, my Uncle Paul moved back home with his mom who is my Aunt Cecelia. I was also living with my aunt at the time so I became an eyewitness to my uncle's disturbing behavior. I was very young but I could tell that something was wrong with him. My Uncle Paul had suffered a lot of mental trauma as a result of the war and he was very angry. It was hard to tell what would set him off but my uncle would often fly into a violent rage. He would get angry and lash out at anything or any person who was next to him. Unfortunately I became his favorite target. My Uncle Paul continuously abused me without mercy. Sometimes the beatings would last for only minutes but other times my Uncle Paul would leave me bloody. As I spent more time at my Aunt Cecelia's house, the beatings became more intense. One time my Uncle Paul beat me so badly that I had to be rushed to the hospital. I remember the entire family becoming angry with my uncle. Even my stepfather, Earl, had to be held back from retaliating against my uncle for what he had done to me. My Uncle Paul had no right to abuse me the way he did. My stepfather wanted to beat my uncle just as bad as he had beaten me. My family convinced my stepfather not to seek revenge against my uncle. After my trip to the emergency room, everyone became aware of what my Uncle Paul had done to me, but no one ever knew the entire story.

For the majority of the time that I stayed at my Aunt Cecelia's house, my Uncle Paul tormented me with nonstop abuse. I never understood why he chose me. I tried my best not to provoke him, but it seemed that there was nothing I could do to prevent his attacks on me. With each passing day Uncle Paul found new ways to abuse me behind closed doors. Once my brother Henry moved into my Aunt Cecelia's home, things became even worse for me.

For as long as I could remember, my brother Henry had bladder issues. He wet the bed a lot when we were kids, so Henry was always permitted to sleep by himself. It was an unwritten rule in my family. If there were only two beds in a room, my brother Henry would sleep by himself and I had to sleep in the bed with my relatives. When my brother moved in with us at my Aunt Cecelia's home, I had to sleep in the bed with my Uncle Paul despite all the mental issues he was experiencing, and all the senseless abuse I was suffering from. It was at that time when my uncle started to take full advantage of me. The scoldings and beatings continued during the day and at night, and the physical abuse became sexual in nature. While everyone else was asleep in the house, my Uncle Paul repeatedly raped me and threatened to punish me further if I ever told my parents.

There aren't enough words I could use to explain how demoralizing and painful it was to be sexually molested by a family member. The dark cloud of confusion, guilt and shame hovered over me for a long time because of my uncle. I wanted to tell anyone who would listen that I was being sexually abused, but I was afraid of the possible consequences. My uncle was very intimidating. There was no question that he struck fear in me. I was barely ten years old and I was experiencing an unnatural violation that no child should be subjected to. Sometimes my uncle would try to justify his actions to me. He would tell me that the *Boogie Man* was doing all those terrible things to me. In a strange way I actually believed that he felt some type of guilt about the physical and emotional assault he was putting me through at such a young and innocent age.

The sexual abuse went on for quite some time. Despite the obvious pain and distress that my uncle was inflicting on me, I could never muster up the courage to put an end to it. An honest conversation with my parents would have quickly ended my nightmare but I was too afraid that my uncle would somehow make things worse for me and my family. I harbored the ugly secret for years, never saying a thing. I was so glad when I finally moved away from Aunt Cecelia and Uncle Paul. My mother never realized that on the day she decided to kidnap me, and make our family whole again, she was actually saving me from the endless abuse that I was suffering from daily. I was finally away from my Uncle Paul and the so-called *Boogie Man* who was consistently attacking me. The physical scars would heal over time but the mental and emotional damage would stay with me well into my adult years. Like many people who survived child abuse, I tried hard to suppress the flashbacks of those dark nights. I didn't want anyone else to know what happened to me so I dealt with the pain alone. I just wanted to go back to being a normal kid. But I would soon learn that my childhood would never be normal again.

A few years after I left my aunt's house, I found out that I would be moving again. This time it would be just for the summer. My father moved out to the west coast with his new wife and he wanted his kids to stay with him during our summer break. My mother agreed to the idea and the Lee children were shipped off to California. Being on a humongous jet for the first time was very exciting. I was about eleven-years old at the time and I couldn't wait to see my dad again. He had started a new life with his new wife who had three children—two girls and one boy. Once I arrived to California with my sister Brigette and my brother Henry, we all joked that we were the Black Brady Bunch.

My dad lived in the northern part of California just outside of Oakland. By the looks of his nice townhome, my father seemed to be doing well with his new family. Their neighborhood reminded me of Virginia but with a lot more fruit trees. My dad had lemons, limes, plums, grapefruits and oranges trees growing in the backyard. I was in heaven. I had never seen anything like it. Back home I was lucky if I found an apple tree or a grapevine. But in California it was an entirely different world. I had never seen so many trees with different fruits growing from them. Back in those days I loved to pick the fresh fruit off the trees and eat it; even when it was not healthy for me.

My dad would always yell at me for eating the fruit. But I could never resist. I stayed in the trees and I stayed getting my butt beat as a result. I remember eating so many plums one day and becoming very ill. I loved sour fruit and the plums I ate that day were green and sour. I was too young to know that green plums were no good for you because they were not ripe. But this particular day I decided to eat the green ones. It was the same day that my dad planned a family trip for us. He loaded everyone into the car and we headed to the very popular San Francisco Zoo. No one had a clue that I wasn't feeling well. They were all excited about the outing. As we approached the front entrance to the zoo, a heavy sickness fell over me. My stomach started hurting bad from the nearly twenty to thirty plums I had eaten earlier. Before we could get out the car and enjoy the trip I started vomiting in the back seat. My brother and sister, along with my step brother and sisters were in the back seat but it didn't matter. I vomited everywhere. Everyone in the car was grossed out and shocked. The vomiting started getting worse and my dad had no choice but to make the decision to go back home. Our trip was ruined. Everyone was angry with me. Unfortunately, we never got a chance to go back to the San Francisco Zoo. But my father and his new wife found different ways to entertain us while we were there in California with them.

I went to my first drive-in cinema when I was on the west coast. Watching a movie from the car was a new experience for me. My family had never gone to a drive-in theater in Maryland, so it was nice to share the experience with Brigette and Henry. If we were not going to the movies or visiting the cool attractions in the area, my siblings and I were getting to know Dad's new family.

While Brigette got closer with our stepsisters, Henry and I hung out with our new stepbrother. He was a few years older than us but he had no problem introducing us to his friends and showing us around. We played sports together and found a lot of things to explore around the neighborhood. I got my first taste of fishing in California. I had never gone fishing before. My stepbrother took us to visit the Berkeley Pier. Lots of kids from the area went to the pier to fish and hang out. We had a blast down there. Making new friends and learning new hobbies made our California trip a lot of fun. And being around my dad again was a bonus. I thought nothing could ruin my summer vacation. While the days I spent on the west coast were filled with fun and adventure, my nights became darker and darker as the summer moved on.

From the moment we pulled up to my father's townhouse in California I noticed that it was a very nice home. But with three additional kids moving into the house there was going to be a challenge trying to keep everyone comfortable. The girls ended up getting their own room to share and Henry and I had to bunk up in my stepbrother's room. Henry was still battling with his bladder issue. He still had the reputation for wetting the bed so he was allowed to sleep by himself. Like always, I had to share the bed with another person and make the best of it. This time that person was my stepbrother. He was much bigger than I was. In fact, his family nicknamed him "Big Boy" because of his enormous size for his age. With the new sleeping arrangements I figured the worse I would have to deal with was not having enough room to sleep comfortably. But I would face a far worse problem that contributed to my restless nights in California.

For the majority of that summer I was repeatedly molested and raped by my stepbrother. Night after night he would wait until everyone was asleep and get on top of me to do his thing. My stepbrother would threaten to beat me up and abuse me even more if I ever told anyone. I never thought the nightmare that I experienced back in my Aunt Cecelia's house would follow me nearly three thousand miles to the west coast. I was once again assaulted and abused by a person who I was taught to love as family. The pain and guilt of the molestation was unbearable. I was burdened with the task of keeping the shameful secret to myself. It seemed as if the abuse continued every night. My brother Henry was a heavy sleeper so I was unsure if he ever knew what was going on inside the bedroom. I wanted to tell my dad on a number of occasions but the fear of my stepbrother had gotten the best of me. No matter how much pain he put me through, I never told a soul about the abuse.

As the summer started to wind down my father decided it was time for us to return to Maryland. Despite the fun times I had on the west coast, I was eager to get away from my stepbrother. I hated the abuse that I was subjected to. I just wanted it to end. Just before the summer was over my father packed the Lee children into his car and decided to take the four-day drive back to Maryland. Unbeknownst to my parents, I was once again whisked away from an abusive family member. There is no telling how much worse off I would have been if I stayed at my dad's house. The physical wounds from those horrific nights in California would heal once again, just like the ones from Aunt Cecelia's house, but the emotional scars would surface throughout my life without warning.

Chapter 6

Fist of Fury

I had mixed emotions about returning to Maryland. I really enjoyed the time I spent in California with my dad and my siblings. I remember the great weather and all the cool new things I tried while I was there. The fruit trees, the fishing, the new friends and all the days of being around Brigette and Henry were priceless. I even entered a dance competition while we were in California and I won first prize. Despite the abuse from my stepbrother, I was able to salvage a number of great memories from that summer on the west coast.

When we returned to Maryland we learned that my mother had made a significant change in her life. Earl and my mother were no longer together and she was living with our next-door neighbor. I was too young to know the whole story but it seemed that they were having major issues. My mother decided it was time to move on from the first father figure in my life. Staying with my biological dad for the summer was the most time I had ever spent with him. Before our trip to California, I only got to see my real dad when he was picking me up or dropping me off at someone else's house. For as long as I could remember, Earl Brooks was my first full-time dad.

Earl was a great provider and he was always good to me. Like my real dad, Earl was a truck driver. He made a decent living and he always made sure that we had everything we wanted. When Christmas came around, Earl would buy everything on our wish list. We got the Huffy Bikes, The Rock'em Sock'em Robots, The Evil Knievel dolls and anything else we asked for. Earl was the biological father of my sister Dawn. For as long as I could remember Earl treated us all like his own children. He was always a perfect dad to me.

53

Earl's family was from Brentwood, Maryland. I was only about five or six years old at the time, but I could remember his entire family always being nice to us back then. They always treated the Lee children with love and made us feel right at home. One of my favorite people from Earl's family was his sister. We called her Aunt Boofy. Every day when I left school I would stop by Aunt Boofy's house before I went home. She would always take care of me when I got there. My fondest memory of Aunt Boofy was being greeted by this incredibly beautiful dark-skinned lady when I arrived from school. She would have a peanut butter and jelly sandwich waiting for me every afternoon. Aunt Boofy would always make my day.

From the outside looking in, the relationship between my mother and Earl was very loving. They cared for each other deeply and anyone watching could tell that their bond was serious. But on some occasions their passion would spill over into a reckless rage. I remember nights when Earl and my mother would have bouts of screaming matches. They would yell and hurl loud insults at each other. The yelling would escalate into physical fighting and things would quickly turn serious. From our bedroom I could hear Earl tussling with my mother. She would throw pots and pans and anything else she could find to back Earl off of her. The thunderous sounds of the brawls would scare me and my siblings. Some nights I would be so afraid that I would hide under the bed and cover my ears. I was scared for my mother. Earl was a big guy. I didn't want him to hurt her but there was nothing I could do. The fighting was always intense. Some nights it sounded like they were going to bring down the entire house.

The domestic violence between my mother and Earl affected me a lot when I was a child. Their relationship confused me because Earl was so good to me. He didn't seem like a bad guy most times. But when he and my mother would have parties at the house it seemed like they would transform into different people. They both drank a lot and the alcohol contributed to their loud altercations. What would start out as a fun card game or friendly gathering would end up as a bar room brawl. I hated when they had those parties. A lot of grown-ups would be in the house and the boisterous gathering would always turn into altercations. If money and liquor was involved in the card games or parties, there was a good chance that a fight would break out before the end of the evening. I later found out that both Earl and my mother had infidelity problems. They were both young and outgoing at the time and most of their arguments were because of unresolved cheating issues. Every fight seemed to get more violent and the fear for my mother's safety grew inside of me. I just didn't want Earl to hurt my mommy.

When we returned from California and I learned that my mother and Earl split, part of me was relieved that my mother would now be safe. I didn't realize it at the time but there was a lot of fire building inside of me from all of the abuse I was witnessing and experiencing in my young life. Between Earl hitting on my mother, my Uncle Paul touching me and being raped by my stepbrother, I was harboring a lot of anger. I wanted badly to defend myself whenever I was attacked back then; and when my mother was fighting with Earl I wanted badly to defend her. Unfortunately, I was powerless in all cases. Now with Earl and my mother no longer living together I was again left with a confusing mix of emotions. I liked Earl as a father and a provider but I hated the violence he unleashed on my mother. It would take some years for me to finally find a way to channel my anger and frustration.

A few years before we made our trip to the west coast my real dad introduced us to one of his high school buddies. His name was Reggie Jackson. He was a Martial Arts instructor and a black belt. My father enrolled Henry and I into Reggie's class to learn Taekwondo and Karate. I was only about seven years old when I started studying the art but I became a huge fan of the lessons. My brother Henry didn't stick with it but I enjoyed it, and wanted to learn more. By the time we made it to California I had already picked up a few valuable moves and techniques. During that fateful summer on the west coast I didn't get a chance to study the art and take classes like I wanted to. I didn't lose total interest in martial arts but there were so many other activities to do. Between the sports, the fishing and the fruit trees I was totally immersed in my summer vacation.

Once my stepbrother started to abuse me I found a new motivation to learn how to defend myself. The nightly assaults scared me but it also made me angry. I wanted revenge on my stepbrother. He was a lot older and a lot bigger than I was back then so I knew I couldn't make him stop his awful behavior. Even when I tried to fight him off I couldn't. I vowed that I would make him pay for all the abuse he put me through. I didn't know how I was going to do it but I told myself that one day I would get him back. I would have never guessed that a movie would inspire me and help change the course of my life.

"Now, you must remember; the enemy has only images and illusions behind which he hides his true motives. Destroy the image and you will break the enemy."

My eyes were wide as saucers as I sat in the back seat of my dad's car. We were watching the epic movie *"Return of the Dragon"* at the drive-in theater. The film starred a young and dynamic martial artist by the name of Bruce Lee. I couldn't believe the amazing styles and movements that he was executing on the large screen. His fighting techniques were flawless and he was a downright badass. As a young kid I couldn't help but believe that Bruce Lee was the type of person that nobody messed with. He could protect himself in any situation and he never allowed himself to be taken advantage of. I wanted to be just like that. I was tired of older boys and men violating me. I wanted to learn how to defend myself just like the great Bruce Lee. From that day I became infatuated with his life and learning Martial Arts.

When I returned to Maryland I was again enrolled in Karate and Taekwondo classes. My mother also signed up Brigette and Henry for the classes, but I was the only one who stuck with it. No one ever knew what my true motivation was. I never missed a class and I concentrated long and hard on all the lessons. I wanted to learn every punch, every kick, every chokehold and every devastating attack to get revenge on my stepbrother. I told myself that if I ever saw him again that he was going to get it. And I meant that.

Before the magic came into my life, learning Karate and studying the great martial artists consumed me. I studied anything that was available about Bruce Lee. I wanted to learn everything I could. He was not only a great Martial Artist but he was also a walking specimen of health. His workout routines and eating habits were legendary. He released dozens of videos of his workout regime. He also shared his diet plans to anyone who was following him. The more I learned about Bruce Lee and his life, the more I wanted to be just like him. I even fantasized about moving to the other side of the world and marrying an Asian woman because of Bruce Lee. My curiosity about the Martial Arts was much more than a passing hobby.

I excelled in all of my Karate and Taekwondo classes. I sparred a lot and even competed in tournaments. I had a lot of rage built up inside of me which helped to ease my learning curve when it came to new techniques. My Karate instructor knew that I fought with an extra chip on my shoulder. He was always impressed with my skills. He nicknamed me "Killer" because he could sense that I was fighting with an extra hot fire burning inside of me. Whenever I would spar against other kids in the class I would imagine that my stepbrother's head was on their body. That small thought would help me channel my anger and focus. Every time I would hit the heavy bag or kick a piece of wood, I would envision hitting my stepbrother. I trained hard because I truly believed that one day I was going to see him again and eventually kick his ass.

I became so good at Martial Arts that I decided to teach other kids in the neighborhood. I turned my backyard into a makeshift dojo and started holding Karate and Taekwondo classes of my own. A lot of kids from the neighborhood wanted to learn how to fight, so they could defend themselves, so they were excited about my classes. I was far from a certified instructor but I had developed a passion for the art of self-defense and I was eager to show off my skills. My backyard was fully equipped with a hanging bag and other equipment for the other kids to use. My classes were based on everything that I had learned from my Karate instructor. Some days I would have ten or more kids training with me. I taught them the basics of how to punch, kick and block. I would wear my uniform and a black belt to let everyone know how good I was. Seven days a week I was in my backyard teaching those classes and becoming better at the craft. Because we shared the same last name my ultimate goal at that time was to be just as good as Bruce Lee.

My obsession with Martial Arts lasted a few years. I always held on to the drive to be a better fighter. I couldn't wait to see my stepbrother again so I could unleash all the fury I had pinned up since the abuse in California. There was only one thing that could take my mind off of the Martial Arts and that was the magic. Once I laid eyes on the magic deck during that infamous television commercial I was immediately thrust onto the path of my lifetime journey. The strong impact of the Martial Arts has never left me. I used the principles of discipline and focus to help me succeed to this very day. Although the magic has since become the dominant force in my life, I never abandoned my infatuation with Bruce Lee and the world of Martial Arts.

Chapter 7

Mr. Sheldon

After splitting up with Earl, my mother's life became all about her children. She always wanted the best for us so she did everything she could to make sure we had a better life. She worked long hours at various companies and soon we found ourselves moving to a better neighborhood. Columbia Park, Maryland was our next stop.

After moving from job to job my mother eventually landed a good paying position at a company called Sheldon Heating and Air Conditioning. The Company was owned by a shrewd businessman by the name of Mr. Sheldon. He was a heavy-set white man who loved food, cigars and making money. He reminded me of a younger version of Jackie Gleason. Mr. Sheldon's heating and air conditioning company was one of the largest in the DMV Area. His company serviced dozens of large office buildings, schools and churches in the region. Mr. Sheldon was serious about his business. He always provided professional service and he was a hawk when it came time to getting paid. But in contract to his business prowess, Mr. Sheldon was also a very sweet man. He loved to enjoy life and put smiles on the faces of the people around him. When my mother began working for his company, Mr. Sheldon was going through a rocky marriage of his own and he was looking for not only a change but happiness.

A few months after she was hired at the company, my mother and Mr. Sheldon started to grow attracted to each other. My mother was a beautiful young woman and Mr. Sheldon found himself falling for her. Their attraction evolved into a love affair and it didn't take long for the news to spread around. Mr. Sheldon was nearly fifteen years older than my mother and all of his kids were adults at the time. His older son was a manager at the heating and air conditioning company and he knew my mother very well. There was never any friction from his kids about Mr. Sheldon falling in love with this attractive young black woman who happened to be my mother. Mr. Sheldon's marriage to his first wife eventually fell apart and things between him and my mother grew serious. Their love for each other matured rapidly and they eventually married. When Mr. Sheldon came into our lives everything changed for the entire family.

By the time my mother married Mr. Sheldon I was becoming more and more interested in the world of magic. I didn't realize it at the time, but Mr. Sheldon actually became very instrumental in helping me on my journey to becoming a professional magician. Mr. Sheldon was always good to me and my siblings. He even hired my brother Henry and my sister Brigette to work at the company. Brigette worked in the front office and Henry ended up learning a number of skills and becoming a sheet metal mechanic. Henry eventually became so well trained in the business that he left Mr. Sheldon's company and started his own business in the area. Henry started off small but he eventually started growing his business and hired other mechanics to work for him. Henry bought his own company truck and started doing business in the DMV area. Mr. Sheldon helped my brother Henry a lot. In fact, Mr. Sheldon helped us all out and we were always grateful.

Mr. Sheldon took a lot of pride in his business. I remember how Mr. Sheldon would drive us around and point out all the buildings that he had serviced. He loved to show us his work as we drove up and down different streets in the area. He once pointed out a large church he had serviced in downtown Washington, DC. The church was owned by a very famous black pastor from the area. Mr. Sheldon told us how the pastor never paid him after he put an air conditioning unit into his church. The pastor was a popular person in the area. He owned a lot of fancy cars and attracted large crowds to his church every Sunday. It was disappointing to hear that Mr. Sheldon had to hunt the pastor down and threatened to sue him. It was an early lesson for me to hear that sometimes Mr. Sheldon never got paid for his work.

One day while I was in his office I noticed a wooden box on Mr. Sheldon's desk. I had seen the box on the desk many times and I was curious as to why it was so important to him. There was a simple caption on the box that read: "HOW TO SUCCEED IN BUSINESS". I asked Mr. Sheldon about the box. He told me to go ahead and open the box if I wanted the answer to the riddle. He smiled at me as I reached down to open the lid. Located inside the box was a metal screwdriver and a flashlight. I grew more confused until I read the caption below. It simply read: "SCREW EVERYBODY." Mr. Sheldon had gotten that advice from his father. That was how Mr. Sheldon was when it came to his business. He was very astute and serious about turning a profit.

When it came to our family Mr. Sheldon was a different person. He was always kind to us. He loved my mother dearly and he wanted nothing but the best for all of us. His business was doing very well back then. When we had to live off my mom's income we lived on a very limited budget, but after Mr. Sheldon came into our lives it seemed like everything changed. He was a very spontaneous person. It was typical for him to load the entire family into the car and take us on trips. One minute we would be home in Maryland, and four hours later we would be on the top of the Empire State Building in New York City. I remember we took a trip to the World Trade Center. My fondest memory of that day was the beautiful blue carpet that covered the top floor of the tower. The view from the large windows was breathtaking. As a child I was always fascinated by the skyscrapers during those trips to New York.

Mr. Sheldon introduced us to another lifestyle. He took us to every type of restaurant he could find. He was not afraid to show us new places to eat nearly every weekend. I remember Mr. Sheldon taking us to one restaurant where they served us frog legs. It was a challenge to get young black kids, who were used to eating hamburgers and pork chops, to now try something as exotic as frog legs. But that was the way Mr. Sheldon was. He was always trying to show us a good time. Because of Mr. Sheldon my family visited some amazing places including the Shenandoah Mountains in Virginia and Radio City Music Hall in New York. We even took a few trips out of the country to Canada.

I never took those trips with my real father. My stepfather Earl was always working and too busy for those long trips so it was good for my family to experience those outings. Mr. Sheldon was always interested in showing us different things. I remember having a picnic with my family in the mountains. A few deer approached us and we fed them fruit directly from our hands. That was something that my siblings and I had never experienced before. From taking long drives to doing something as simple as a picnic, Mr. Sheldon always tried to help us see new things and new places, and eat new foods.

The best thing about Mr. Sheldon was the fact that he and my mother were in love. They were genuinely happy together. After a while we moved out of Columbia Park, Maryland and moved to a better neighborhood. There were always five or six cars in the driveway and our house was always furnished with nice things. I remember watching the Motown 25 Special when Michael Jackson showed the world the moonwalk dance. Our entire family watched that special in the den of our nice home. That was one of the many special moments I remember sharing with my family and Mr. Sheldon.

Life was so different with Mr. Sheldon. There were always keys to a car in our house. My older brother had a license but I was too young to drive. Mr. Sheldon told us that we could drive any of the cars as long as we had a license. There was one exception. Mr. Sheldon had one prized possession that sat in our driveway. It was a black Pontiac Trans Am. Mr. Sheldon told us that we could drive any car except his black sports car with the tinted T-tops. He loved that car. He was inspired to buy the vehicle from a famous movie called Smokey and the Bandit starring Burt Reynolds and Sally Fields. One day while he and my mother were on vacation in the Pocono Mountains, my brother and I decided to take the Trans Am for a spin. We drove the car down to DC just to take it around for a joy ride. We got the car back in one piece and we made sure we put the keys back where we found them. We knew there would be hell to pay if Mr. Sheldon ever found out that we took his car for an extended test drive.

Looking back I can honestly say that it never felt weird that my mother was in an interracial relationship with Mr. Sheldon. He seemed to fit right in with our family. He would go to all of our family functions, including reunions, and he even went to church with us. He never tried to act black or try too hard to blend in with us. He had a warm and genuine personality. Mr. Sheldon was just himself and we loved him for that. When he wasn't working or taking us on trips, he was always telling jokes. Mr. Sheldon was a big joke-teller; he was the king of the one-liners. He was a very funny person who always kept us laughing. If you were around Mr. Sheldon you were going to hear some jokes. Most of them would start with the famous line *"You ever hear the one about..."* Mr. Sheldon was a walking joke book. That was just part of his personality. He always tried to make the people around him happy.

I always thought about how Mr. Sheldon seemed to come around at the perfect time. As I became more intrigued about the business of magic I wanted to learn as much as I could. Mr. Sheldon was very instrumental to my early career as a magician. When it was time for me to take more classes on the subject it was Mr. Sheldon who paid for my magic lessons. He made sure that I got all of the materials I needed to continue learning my craft. Mr. Sheldon knew that the magic would keep me out of trouble. He recognized that I was interested in the art and he wanted to make sure that I stuck with it. He never wanted me to quit. Later on when I booked my birthday party gigs, it was Mr. Sheldon who helped me get to ninety percent of my shows. I didn't have a driver's license at the time and Mr. Sheldon would make sure I got to my jobs and made sure I got there on time. Week after week Mr. Sheldon would sit in the car while I did a magic show or took my magic classes. He was a big eater so most days he would grab himself a sandwich and relax in his car while I handled my business. He never complained or made me feel bad about driving me around. He wanted me to succeed.

Mr. Sheldon's impact on my life was invaluable. Even the smallest things he did for me had a huge affect on my life and my career. He was the first person to drive me around Potomac, Maryland and show me the nice houses and the affluent neighborhoods. He told me to aspire to be rich so that I could afford to live in those types of neighborhoods. He always told me to have large dreams.

I'm not sure how much of a career I would have had without Mr. Sheldon. In addition to paying for my magic lessons and materials, Mr. Sheldon was the person who took me to see the great magician, Harry Blackstone. Mr. Sheldon was the one who took me to all the Broadway shows in New York. He opened my mind to a larger world of entertainment. When it was time to take those long drives to Virginia to do my magic shows, Mr. Sheldon never hesitated to jump in his car and drive me to my gigs. No matter how long the shows were, Mr. Sheldon would wait patiently in his car and allow me to work and help grow my business. Sometimes I would do two shows a day and Mr. Sheldon would be right there. He helped me load up the station wagon with all of my props and rabbits and he never asked me for gas money. If it wasn't for Mr. Sheldon, I have no clue how I would have been able to do so many birthday parties back then and brand my name. My mother didn't have a car at the time and my brother was unable to drive. Without Mr. Sheldon it is very possible that I wouldn't have built my magic business so quickly. He knew how to get to all of my events because he was familiar with the DMV area. Before mobile phones and GPS, Mr. Sheldon was skilled at finding all of the addresses and getting me to my events on time. Even as my name began to circulate and my bookings increased, Mr. Sheldon let me use one of his offices to make calls and follow up on my events. He was just a really good person.

As I moved away from the birthday parties and started to transition to a different style of magic I started to see less and less of Mr. Sheldon. I began to do more juggling and street performing, so my birthday party business started to die out. When it was time for me to do my events I took the metro train and hung out with my friends who had cars. I was about sixteen when I started hanging with my good friend Chris and we did a lot of events and festivals together. As I spent less time at home I didn't see a lot of Mr. Sheldon. He and my mother started taking more trips and enjoying their lives together. My mom and Mr. Sheldon were very good for each other. They were madly in love and anyone who knew them could see that they were a perfect match. My mom always made sure that his business ran smooth and that Mr. Sheldon was happy. Even when he fell ill my mother tried her best to keep his company growing. Mr. Sheldon's poor diet and smoking had caught up to him a number of years later. He became very sick and could no longer run his business. I was disheartened when I learned that a number of people started to take advantage of him. Some customers stopped paying their bills and even the people who worked for him started to pinch off of him. His business eventually folded as Mr. Sheldon struggled with his health.

One night my mother called me crying and distraught on the other line. It was hard for her to break to news to me and I could barely make out her words. My mom had been taking care of Mr. Sheldon for a number of years but his health began to rapidly decline. A decision had been made to move Mr. Sheldon to a nursing home so that he could receive care around the clock. My mother would visit Mr. Sheldon every day. As she cried on the phone to me I knew something bad happened. My mother told me that she had seen Mr. Sheldon earlier that day. She said that she massaged his legs and that he was in good spirits. Before she left him, she gave him a kiss goodbye not realizing that she would never see him alive again. Later that evening, actually in the middle of the night, Mr. Sheldon woke up. He asked one of the nurses for a glass of water. The nurse walked out of the room and when she returned Mr. Sheldon had passed away peacefully in his bed. The news devastated us all.

I had never heard my mother so broken up. She loved Mr. Sheldon and the loss created ripple effects throughout our family. Mr. Sheldon was so kind and loving to his family and he was never afraid to show his emotions. It is hard for me to imagine what kind of person I would be if Mr. Sheldon would have never entered our lives. He was very giving and before meeting him I had never experienced the things he willingly shared with us from the kindness of his heart. Mr. Sheldon is truly a person I owe a great deal of my success to. I'm so grateful that my mother welcomed him to our family.

Chapter 8

Happy 18th Birthday

L ooking back on my teenage years I often wonder how I was ever able to meet new friends. Despite my growing magic career, I continued to be a very shy kid as I entered my high school years. I was very outgoing when I would hang around my boys from the neighborhood, but when it was time to talk to the girls in my school I would always clam up. It was like I had two personalities. I was a very popular kid in high school by I was very shy when it came to the girls. I always wanted to entertain my peers and most of my teachers knew me as a class clown. It didn't take long for that reputation to stick to me. Most of the kids knew who I was and there were a few girls who wanted to ask me out. I never got to know the ones who were too scared to approach me. I always feared rejection, so I would never make the first move. I only got to know the girls in my school that were brave enough to spark up a conversation with me.

When I was around my boys I was a total different person. I knew a lot of fellas from the neighborhood, but our crew was very tight. I mainly hung around three guys—my good friends Bruce, Eric and Kenny. We thought we were just like the boys from the Cooley High movie. Like all typical friends back then, we did everything together. Some days we played basketball and hung out at the gym, and other days we hung out at my house or down at the park. I was always the ring leader of the bunch. I was the loudest and the baddest. I was always the one to get into trouble first. No matter the circumstance, I was the first one ready to fight. If someone was messing with my friends I would be the first one ready to rumble. I had no problem being the leader.

When it came to girls however, I was a late bloomer. My boys were all players and they had multiple girlfriends. They would always brag about making out with girls and doing all sorts of things with them. I couldn't participate in most of the conversations because I was still a virgin. I never told my boys how inexperienced I was. My friends even tried to hook me up with a few girls from school. When things would get hot and heavy with the opposite sex, I didn't know what to do next. I never told the girls that I was green as a cucumber when it came to sex. Because of my shyness I held on to my virginity throughout most of my high school years.

One day I was making out with one of my girlfriends under the stairway inside the school. I was feeling all over her body and she was insisting that we have sex. I became nervous and couldn't bring myself to do it. Needless to say, our relationship didn't last much longer. That was how the majority of my high school flings came and went. Most of my girlfriends were the aggressive type. Although they were young they were always faster than I was. They seemed to be more experienced and more than ready to fool around. It took a while for me to get up the nerve to finally take that leap and become a man. I didn't know it at the time but it would take a late night encounter to help me get over my shyness and finally lose my virginity.

During the middle of that school year I started dating a really pretty girl named Lolita. She transferred from another district and she was fresh on the scene. Not long after she arrived, Lolita became known as the hot girl in the school. All of the boys wanted her, but she had eyes for me. I was too scared to approach her and one day she let me know that she had a crush on me. Because of the magic career, I started off really slow when it came to dating Lolita. I knew she liked me, but my game wasn't up. I had a bad rap game; I honestly didn't know how to talk to girls and had no clue what they wanted to hear. Lolita had to do all the work. It was hard for me to initiate contact or even spark up a meaningful conversation. She definitely booked me because I was too scared to book her. After a few months of dating it became apparent that Lolita wanted more from me than just an occasional kiss and a hug.

I was living in Largo, Maryland at that time. We lived in an upper class neighborhood named Kettering. My mother and Mr. Sheldon were married and we were living in a really nice housing community. All of my siblings were still living at home as well. A few months into that school year my mother and Mr. Sheldon allowed me to have a party at the house to celebrate my eighteenth birthday. I invited all of my friends over and of course I asked my girlfriend Lolita to come. Despite the fact that I was performing magic for dozens of birthday parties, this was the first time I actually had a birthday party of my own as a teenager. We had a lot of food and there was real music being played. All of my friends were partying in the basement and making out when my parents were not around. My mother and Mr. Sheldon were really cool about my party. They allowed us to have our privacy and actually wanted everyone to have a good time.

The party went on late into the evening until everyone finally started to trickle out and head home to beat their curfews. As the party started to end, my girlfriend Lolita let me know that she didn't have a ride home. I didn't have a car so I asked my mother if Lolita could spend the night at our house. My mother agreed and told me that Lolita could sleep on the couch in the basement. She said she would take Lolita home in the morning. My room was also in the basement, so I thought it would be cool to have my girlfriend sleeping in the room just next door to me.

Shortly after all of my friends left, except Lolita, my mother cleaned up the house a bit and then headed off to bed. I kissed my girlfriend goodnight as she got comfortable on the couch. I made sure she was fine, then I went into my bedroom and closed the door. Although everyone else in the house went to sleep, Lolita obviously had other plans. She didn't stay on the sofa the entire night. In fact, she waited until she was sure everyone was sound asleep and she slipped into my room and got into the bed with me.

It didn't take long for things to escalate once Lolita got in my bed. One thing led to another and eventually we both were getting naked and exploring each other like the curious teenagers we were. I didn't tell Lolita that I was a virgin. She naturally took the lead and initiated everything. I could tell that she was experienced. Lolita made my first sexual encounter amazingly memorable. I had no clue what I was doing that night, but I pretended the whole way through. Lolita was a fast girl from the DC area. She had no problems making the first move on me. If she wasn't the aggressive type I would have never lost my virginity on my 18th birthday. I was clearly attracted to her, but I was always nervous to speak up and tell her what I wanted. I'm sure Lolita grew tired of waiting decided to take matters into her own hands…*literally*.

After losing my virginity that night in the basement, I did what most men do after they make love. I fell asleep. Instead of getting back on the couch, Lolita cuddled with me. It felt good to have her naked body next to me. We both drifted off to sleep and spent the entire night together in each other's arms.

"HEY, Y'ALL WAKE UP!!!"

The familiar voice shook me out of my sleep. I immediately opened my eyes and noticed my mother was standing at the foot of my bed. It was the crack of dawn and I quickly realized that I slept the entire night away. My heart dropped to my stomach. I looked over and noticed that Lolita was still in the bed with me, and we both were naked. I was beyond embarrassed. I scrambled to cover up. I just knew my mother was going to kill me. Lolita jumped to her feet and began to grab her clothes. My mother turned around and headed back upstairs. My heart was beating so fast and hard that it felt like it was going to jump out of my chest. I couldn't believe that the entire night slipped by and it was already morning. A million thoughts ran through my mind. I could only imagine what my mother was going to say about us having sex in her house.

Lolita showered and dressed. About twenty minutes later, Lolita left the basement and went upstairs to wait for my mother to take her home. I stayed in my room for a few minutes to gather my thoughts. I knew I had to face my mother after being caught, not only naked with my girlfriend, but in my bed in my parents house. My level of embarrassment was indescribable. I knew I had to face the music sooner or later so after a few anxious minutes I decided it was time to leave my room.

When I got upstairs my mother was in the kitchen cooking. Lolita was helping her and there was a thick silence in the air. I was trying to think of something to say to my mother to ease the tension. Nothing came to mind. I knew my girlfriend was nervous and embarrassed, so she stayed quiet. When my mother noticed me in the kitchen she turned to look at Lolita, and gave her a peculiar look.

"Hey, what are you doing shacking up with my son?" My mother asked.

There was a moment of uncomfortable silence until my mother chuckled and a wide grin came across her face. I was shocked that she wasn't furious. Instead it was like my mother was amused at what she'd just witnessed in the basement. To my relief there was no drama that morning. My mother was cool, and she never made my girlfriend feel bad. I'm not sure if my mother ever knew that I lost my virginity during that night with Lolita. I was thankful that she was cool about catching us in the bed together.

After we ate breakfast my mother kept her promise and dropped Lolita off at home. During entire ride to Lolita's house my mother made small talk with us and never once made us feel ashamed or fearful about what happened after the party. It was a special day for me that turned into a special night and I can only assume that my mother didn't want to spoil the experience. After she dropped off Lolita my mother never mentioned that morning.

Later that year Lolita left Maryland. She transferred to another school district in Washington, DC and we eventually went our separate ways. I had a few more girlfriends in high school, after Lolita, and most of them were just as aggressive. I never got over my shyness during those years. I have to believe that if Lolita had never made the first move on me, I probably would have held on to my virginity for a few more years.

Nearly a decade went by before I saw Lolita again. We bumped into each other while I was visiting DC. We were both in our late twenties at the time. She was still very attractive, but I could tell that the fast life was getting the best of her. Lolita was always a fast talker and more mature than a lot of the kids in our school. As she got older it seemed that her lifestyle may have been dealing her a few bad hands. We talked for a couple of minutes and once again we went our separate days. They say that everyone will always remember their first time and with Lolita I agree with that notion. She will always hold a special place in my memory.

Chapter 9

Time To "Stand Up"

A s I matured into my late teens the hunger to expand my career intensified. I was no longer infatuated with simply being a magician and entertaining fans of illusions. The vision of becoming a greater performer became very real for me. I began to chase something more...something bigger. I wanted to create a unique act that no one had ever seen before. In my search to create the ultimate stage show, I discovered the exciting and explosive world of Stand-Up Comedy.

Once my mind was made up it didn't take long for me to start earning my stripes as a stand-up comic. In fact, I didn't have to travel far. Washington, DC was grooming some of the most talented acts in the country at the time. Comedic stars like Martin Lawrence, Dave Chappelle and Wanda Sykes all built a name for themselves by coming up in the ranks of comedians in the DMV area. It was an exciting time for all of us as we rotated from stage to stage and worked on our performances. There were dozens of open-mic-nights every week. From Garvin's Comedy Club to The Comedy Café, there was no shortage of locations throughout the area where a young up-and-coming comic could get a few minutes on stage to shine. But not all of the stages were friendly.

As I searched for open-mics and comedy clubs where I could perform, one of my friends suggested I check out Ibex Nightclub. The venue was known for having a tough audience. But after a few shows I became a regular there. Because of the rugged nature of the audience, all of the comics called Ibex Nightclub the Apollo Theater of Washington, DC. It was almost impossible for any comedian to last a full set without being heckled. The club was notorious for making the comedians perform just before a large band was set to light up the stage. The club owner would schedule most comedians to open for a famous artist like Chuck Brown or even a legendary act like The Delfonics. Ibex Nightclub was an old and dingy spot that sat on the corner of Georgia and Missouri Avenues in the northwest section of the city. The club catered to an older crowd who loved to come out and support the musical talents that graced the stage. There was no question that the headliners ruled the vibe. Most young comics wouldn't survive the cold reception they would receive during their act. It was a nightmare. Even the best of us had a terrible fifteen minutes on the Ibex stage. It was a rough place to do comedy but I learned a lot from those days. I figured if I could survive Ibex, I could perform anywhere.

Making those weekly rounds to the different clubs and venues throughout the area helped me improve my act. It also helped me with the branding of my name. I always used props and magic in my shows so the noise about my style of comedy started to buzz around the circuit. I tried to find any stage in the area to showcase my fifteen minutes. By the time I set my sights on the comedy scene I had already dropped the name *LeeDini The Magician*. It was time for me to elevate my game. I knew I had to introduce my act to as many people as I could. I was determined to make fans across the world remember the name Kevin Lee.

In addition to performing at the nightclubs, I entered any comedy competition I could find. I was never afraid of putting my skills to the test against any comic. I competed and won a number of events at The Comedy Café in those days. Crowds and judges throughout the competitions always found the novelty of my act refreshing. I never wanted to resemble any comic that was around. My goal was to always be better.

During my search for more competitions, I was put on to a show at the *LaMaze Nightclub* in Washington, DC. The show was billed as a comedy competition with a cash prize. Once I got wind of the show I immediately signed up to be a part of it. There were about six comedians added to the show including an up-and-coming comedian by the name of Tommy Davidson. I had heard of Tommy around the circuit but we had never performed on the same stage. Tommy was building his name in the urban comedy market. A lot of Hip-Hop fans knew of Tommy back then because he had a bit in his set where he paid homage to the famous rap group known as The Fat Boys. Tommy had a beat-boxing routine that kept the audiences rolling. When it was time for the competition, I knew I had to be on my A-game if I wanted to take home the prize.

As fate would have it, I not only performed well that evening but I won the entire competition. I won first place and Tommy Davidson won second place. I felt a strong sense of accomplishment with winning first place at the *LaMaze Nightclub*. That evening gave me more confidence and helped to boost my drive to keep going. Like most people during that time, Tommy and the rest of the comedians had never seen anything like my act and they always complimented me. I had been performing for dozens of crowds before I hit the comedy scene so my act was solid and very well put together. Most times my act was even more polished than the comedians who were older than me.

Tommy and I eventually became friends and we have crossed paths a number of times throughout our careers. Tommy continued to be successful around the DMV area. He went from performing his act at urban strip clubs to becoming a television star in the mid-80s. His big break came when the R&B legend Anita Baker performed at an afterparty at Ibex Nightclub. Anita Baker saw Tommy's act and decided to take him on tour with her. Tommy appeared on the Arsenio Hall show, and later became one of the featured cast members on Fox's hit television show *In Living Color*. Anytime that Tommy and I speak, it's difficult not to bring up those roughs days back then. We reminisce about performing in those smoky clubs in the nation's capital. We are always amazed at how far our careers have come. Tommy never hesitates to tell me how much he appreciates the advice and lessons we both shared with each other back then.

After taking home the trophy that night from the LaMaze competition I started contacting more clubs and expanding my network. I was ready to hit the road and take my act outside of the DMV area. About a year after becoming a professional comic I did exactly what I knew I was ready for. I secured bookings in various cities and hit the road. I became connected to a popular booking agent in Philadelphia by the name of Andy Scarpetti. He hired me to work the comedy circuit throughout the Philadelphia and southern New Jersey area. Another booking agent I worked with was a guy by the name of Joey Nowak. He had visited the Garvin's Comedy Club in Washington, DC and saw my act. He was very impressed with my performance and immediately hired me to work the New York circuit. I quickly became very busy and being on the road as a stand-up comic became a regular thing for me. New York and Philadelphia have always been hot markets for comedy and entertainment. Being on those stages helped create a buzz for *Kevin Lee* and soon other agents from other markets started calling.

If the agents were not calling me I would call and make contact with them. I was a serious go-getter and I always hustled to secure bookings. I made calls, sent packages, sent faxes and even harassed people into booking me at various venues. I knew I was good at my craft but I had to introduce and re-introduce myself to dozens of agents to make sure I stayed busy. My package eventually landed on the desk of an agent who had contacts out in the Minnesota area. It didn't take long for me to get booked there. My first gig in the area was at a venue called The First Avenue Club and that gig became the start of an amazing rollercoaster ride that took me all over the world.

On August 3, 1983, musical legend Prince was working on his sixth solo album. The amazing writer, composer and vocalist recorded his album "*Purple Rain*" in front of a live audience at the world famous First Avenue Club. For the lucky people who were in attendance that evening, they had no clue that Prince would debut an amazing project that would live forever in the halls of musical lore. As a huge Prince fan, it was an honor to perform on the same stage that was made famous by the musical icon and his diamond-selling album and movie. I performed at the First Avenue Club a few years later after Prince blessed the world with Purple Rain. I opened for an R&B group named *Ready For the World*. They were famous for their hit record "*Oh Sheila*."

I did a few shows in the area and eventually performed at a spot called The Comedy Corner in Milwaukee. Working in Milwaukee at The Comedy Corner was quite the experience. I was a long way from Palmer Park, Maryland. The people were a lot different out there but they always loved my act. The agent I was working with would have all of the working comics stay in a condo near the venue to save on hotel cost. Every week a different comic would fly into Milwaukee and stay in the rented condo. The manager would leave the key under the rug and ask that we replace it once we left.

When I arrived at the condo I was very impressed with the building. It was in a nice neighborhood and I felt excited to be in a new area. Being on the road as a working comic was always fun and I was ready for another excellent weekend. When I walked to the front entrance I looked under the rug. As promised the key was left for me. I keyed into the condo and walked inside.

I immediately noticed that something was strange. There were clothes and bags everywhere in the living room. The condo was plush but it looked lived in. There were socks, underwear, pants, shirts and shoes tossed everywhere. I started to think that I had arrived on the wrong weekend.

A few minutes later a tall man emerged from the back bedroom. He was shirtless and had a small towel wrapped around his waist. He was coolly smoking on a cigarette and didn't seem at all surprised that I was there. I immediately recognized him. It was Andrew Dice Clay.

Dice had just finished a movie called "*Pretty In Pink.*" He was far from a household name at the time but plenty of fans across the country knew who he was. They loved his raunchy comedy routines and Dice was poised to become a huge success. Clay walked up to me and introduced himself. He was very down to earth and cool. His girlfriend was also there in the condo with him. She was basically naked as she walked out of the bedroom. Dice seemed to be unfazed by the fact that she was walking around nude in front of me.

"So, you are the comedian I'm working with this weekend?" Clay asked me as we shook hands.

"Yes," I replied.

Dice and I were both on the bill for the next few days. We hung out all weekend in-between the shows. He was also with his partner from Los Angeles named Hot Tub Johnny. Dice sometimes referred to Johnny as his sidekick and sometimes as his business manager. They both loved to have fun and enjoy themselves when Dice was not on stage. Hanging with Dice showed me another side of the stand-up comedy world. He was loved everywhere he went. Dice was not only an excellent performer but he was one hell of a stand-up comic. He commanded respect on the stage and he didn't like for anyone to interrupt his flow. Sometimes his raunchy and dominant side got him into trouble.

The weekend I worked with Andrew Dice Clay was supposed to be a four day run with Dice closing the shows. After a few nights, the audiences began to grow surlier as the weekend arrived. One night a heckler would not stop interrupting Dice's show. She would blurt out insults and try to knock Dice off of his game. It worked. Dice got fed up. His temper got the best of him. The woman refused to be respectful to Dice's routine so the crude comedian decided to fire back.

"Here's to you sucking my dick," Dice coolly blurted into the microphone.

Dice held up his glass like he was proposing a toast. Before the lady could react, Dice hurled the glass at the woman and spilled the liquor all over her. Everyone in the comedy club was shocked by Dice's move. Some people laughed and others were in pure disbelief. Andrew Dice Clay was fired by the club that evening. I ended up closing out the rest of the weekend and I had killer shows. Dice's dismissal led to a great opportunity for me. My agent back in the south heard amazing reviews about my set and the club booked me to return to the area. This time I would not have to worry about opening for anyone. I was the headliner. For the first time in my career I was the closing act for an upscale comedy club.

During my second comedic-run in Milwaukee I was the co-headliner with a woman named Diana Jordan. She was a seasoned comedian out of Los Angeles. She was a very funny lady who kept the audiences laughing at The Comedy Corner. Diana and I talked a lot during that week-long run. She introduced me to a few people from an advertising agency representing the Miller Brewing Company. Some of the executives had come out to watch her performance. They were fascinated by her show and informed her that they were putting together a comedy tour overseas. It was called The Miller Comedy Tour. The tour would take place primarily on the military bases and the surrounding regions throughout the world. While they were at The Comedy Corner, the executives from the agency had also seen my act. Diana put in a good word for me, and then my agent made it happen. Before I left Milwaukee, I was officially added to the tour.

The Miller Comedy Tour was an amazing opportunity for me. The agency seemed to have an unlimited budget to help promote the Miller brand and also support the troops. I didn't know it at the time but the Miller Comedy Tour would keep me flying in and out of the country for nearly five years. The main purpose was to promote the beer brand and bring comedy to the soldiers who were deployed overseas. A few months later I was packing my things and heading out of the country for my first three-week tour run.

Being on the Miller Comedy Tour was like something out of a movie. It was the first time I flew first class on a Boeing 747. I stayed in five-star hotels and I ate like a king in every place we landed. We were all treated like world class stars on this tour. They pampered us and made sure we were well taken care of. Everything was paid for and the only thing we had to buy was our clothes and souvenirs. Although we performed on the military bases, we normally stayed in the finest hotels in the area. We made stops in Italy, Spain, German and London just to name a few of the finer locations.

Along with Diana Jordan, Marty Levenstein was added to the tour. The agency alternated five comics throughout the year but I was never replaced. Throughout the entire tour run I was the only African-American comic on the bill. It was an exciting time for me as a young comic. Given the opportunity to tour the world to perform was nothing short of a thrill ride. I learned a lot about the world and also I learned a lot about the business.

Before selling the company in 2002, Miller Beer was owned by the global cigarette giant Phillip Morris. One of the first tricks I dazzled my audiences with was an anti-smoking joke in which I would make a lit cigarette disappear. I performed that trick hundreds of times before I was hired by the Miller Comedy Tour. The bit would get such a great response that I decided to use the trick on the tour. The soldiers loved the illusion. One day an executive from Milwaukee flew out to one of the tour stops to check in on the performances. He saw my disappearing cigarette bit and became furious. I was asked to immediately drop the bit from my show. The Milwaukee agency was fearful that the anti-smoking joke would cause a business conflict with Phillip Morris. That was the first time I learned about the power of my show and how a small joke could affect thousands of people.

As the tour dates continued to pour in, it seemed that the locations became larger and more interesting. We performed on Battleships at times in the middle of the vast oceans. Before the performances we were taken on tours of the ships. We got a firsthand account of how the soldiers were living, working and defending our country. One location that will always stand out to me is Korea. During the tour we performed on the Osan Air Base in South Korea. The Osan Air Base is where the legendary Martial Artist Chuck Norris was raised. Because I was a huge fan of martial arts I was excited to perform at the base.

Once we were done at the Osan Air Base we were taken to the border of North Korea and South Korea called the Demilitarized

Zone. We did not stay in a fancy hotel during that part of the tour. We stayed on the military base. It was very scary performing on that base because we were just a few miles from a tense standoff. We were told that if a war broke out between South Korea and North Korea, the life expectancy for everyone within spitting distance of the DMZ would be just a few seconds. It felt good to make the soldiers laugh during those anxious evenings. Keeping their minds off the grim reality of an impending war was a special duty that all the comedians took pride in.

Being an American in South Korea, at that time, made you stand out like a celebrity. But being an American male in South Korea made you a target. Not a target for violence or kidnapping but a target for the prostitutes. It seemed that there was no shortage of available working girls no matter what part of the country we performed in. Once we arrived at our hotel the prostitutes were never far away. It was not uncommon to receive a knock on your door just minutes after you checked into your room. Some of the bellmen were undercover pimps who would watch us comedians as we arrived and would send the girls directly to our rooms.

During most of the tour dates we were assigned a guide to show us around. Mr. Hue was one of our coolest Korean guides. He was assigned to help us navigate the cities and make sure we had everything we needed. He would take us to the markets, restaurants and bars to keep us entertained. He even took us to the bath houses where the Korean women would bathe us and offer up massages. I had never seen anything like it. Mr. Hue was the guide that introduced me to Itaewon. The popular shopping district is a very unique place in Seoul, Korea. It was in Itaewon where I had my first suit made. The seamstress measured me as I chose the colors and materials and thirty minutes later an entire suit was sewn together for me and was ready to wear. It was wild. If you were a fan of knock-off bags and clothes, Itaewon was your place. They had everything. And the prices were insanely low. Like always, the American dollar stretched a mile over in Korea. All of us would buy new shoes, bags, colognes and jewelry and take it back to the states.

Guam was another stop we made during The Miller Comedy Tour. I remember the beautiful water surrounding the island. It was in that water where I snorkeled for the first time. It was such a fantastic experience. One day when I was finished snorkeling I came back to my hotel room. I was preparing for another night of fun in the region when I decided to take a shower. I headed into the bathroom and pulled back the shower curtain. I almost jumped out of my skin when I discovered a snake curled up in the bottom of the bathtub. I almost had a heart attack because of my terrible fear of snakes.

Guam is notorious for its snake problem. When the American military bases first opened in Guam, there was a growing issue with the rodents on the island. A program was started to increase the snake population and even today there is a major snake problem in Guam. During my stay in Guam I witnessed entirely too many snake fights at bars and restaurants throughout the island. I once watched a mongoose fight a snake to the death. A mongoose will rarely lose to a snake. One night I watched a mongoose kill a snake and after the match the chef made snake tea out of the loser. I had my first taste of snake tea while in Guam.

Traveling throughout the region with this tour was a life changing experience for me. Visiting the exotic places and experiencing the different cultures was very enlightening. I remember traveling around and wearing my black leather jacket with the American flag on the back of it. The sleeves were red, white and blue. It gave me a sense of pride to be an American. I walked the streets of Rota, Spain, Tokyo, Japan and Seoul, Korea with that jacket on. Things were different in the 80s. You didn't have to worry about somebody kidnapping you or killing you because you were wearing the American flag. We felt safe in most places where we traveled. People treated us well. It was nothing for the comics to leave the hotel in one city and hop in a cab to travel and see the sights. Nobody bothered us. It was a different time.

People love to laugh. No matter what color they are or where they live. One night I was performing for an audience in Okinawa, Japan. Most of the people were Asian and they loved my show. They were cracking up laughing and everyone had a good time.

After the show, one of the men approached me with a huge smile on his face. "That is amazing," the man said.

"What is amazing?" I questioned.

"They were cracking up laughing at your jokes and none of them speak English." He laughed.

Hearing that made me feel even more proud of my act. To break through the language barrier and have people enjoy my show was a very humbling experience that I will never forget.

Traveling and performing with the Miller Comedy Tour was the best time in my life. I traveled to dozens of military bases throughout the world and performed for thousands of troops. I performed in the deserts of Bahrain in the Middle East and remember picking up metal shards from the scud missiles that Sadaam Hussain dropped on the country. I performed on the military bases in Germany and I remember hanging out with Miss Germany during our stay. I have traveled to military bases in the Hawaiian Islands, Iceland, London and the Mediterranean region. I was young and enjoying life. I was paid handsomely to do what I loved to do. I was also performing for the best crowds throughout the world. Because the men and women of the military didn't get to see much state-side entertainment while they were deployed, they enjoyed themselves very much when The Miller Comedy Tour came around.

When I was younger I had always envisioned traveling overseas and performing in front of sold-out crowds. When I was practicing my magic tricks in the basement I would fantasize about being a global star and having people from all walks of life enjoy my set. To travel to all four corners of the world to perform was a personal fantasy since I discovered my love for magic. The Miller Comedy Tour was nothing short of a dream come true. During one of my breaks I returned home for a few weeks. An article was written about me in The Washington Post. They referred to me as "The New Bob

Hope" because I was entertaining the troops. I couldn't have received a more generous honor. When people ask me what was the best time of my career, it is hard to top my experience of entertaining the brave soldiers of our military. It is a time in my life I will always cherish and the memories will last forever.

Chapter 10

It's Showtime

There is and always has been an ugly stereotype given to the black entertainment world. For the longest time I was considered a "mainstream" comic because of my various tour stops and the comedy clubs I performed in. The difference of the labels is very simple. If you perform in front of a predominantly white audience, you are considered a mainstream performer. And if you perform for a black audience you are thrown into a category referred to as the "chittlin circuit." The derogatory phrase has been used since the early 19th century to describe all the black clubs, bars, studios, stages and venues where the black people frequented and performed. The stereotype has persisted throughout the years and during the early 90s I became fully aware of how that label could destroy a performer's career.

Soon after I had returned from performing overseas for the military I wanted to resume my road gigs and perform in comedy clubs and colleges. I was ready to add more work to my plate so I contacted a big-time agent out of Atlanta. This was during the time when there was no email so I had to snail mail a package to him. I was on the grind and serious about booking more performances. The agent was well plugged into the comedy circuit. He booked a lot of talent for dozens of comedy clubs and venues throughout the country. Just from reviewing my package he could tell that I was hungry. The agent immediately added me to his roster and booked me a lot of gigs. I was booked to work with Andrew Dice Clay and eventually I was scheduled to be the opening act for the very talented and popular actor/comedian Sinbad.

Soon after signing the contract with the Agent, I found myself on the road and performing various nights with Sinbad. His brother Mark was his road manager and we all became very cool. I was rocking red hair back then and a lot of people said that I looked like a skinny Sinbad. I wasn't offended by the comparison. After all, it was an honor to be on the road with him. Night after night we would head to a new town and we would have the audiences rolling. It was a great experience for me as a young comic.

When Sinbad was not on the road and performing at the comedy clubs he was hosting a show called *"Showtime at the Apollo"*. The televised show aired on NBC every Saturday night at 11:30pm est. Sinbad and I had discussed the possibility of me making an appearance on the show. *Showtime at the Apollo* featured a number of celebrity guests including James Brown, Pattie LaBelle, Run D.M.C., Boyz II Men, MC Hammer and hundreds of others. The show was also famous for its amateur night segment. Everyone that watched *"Showtime at the Apollo"* knew that the amateur night segment was a hard draw for any performer. During this portion of the show the audience had a chance to voice their approval or disapproval of an act by cheering or booing during their performance. The legendary Apollo Theater had a reputation of making and breaking an artist whenever they graced the stage.

The Apollo audience was a tough crowd. If they loved you they would cheer you on. But if they didn't like your set, they would boo you and call you out until the *Sandman* jumped on stage and escorted you off to the sound of loud jeering and insults. Even when an artist was a main act the Apollo crowd would unleash their fury on them. During one infamous performance, the R&B legend Barry White was booed by the crowd in the middle of his set. The Apollo crowd could be relentless no matter who you were.

I was conflicted about the possibility of performing on the show. I told Sinbad that I was unsure of how well my act would play in front of an all-black audience. For most of my career I had performed for white crowds both overseas and in the states. I wasn't sure if a black audience would like a set that was composed of half magic and half comedy. Sinbad totally disagreed with me. He told me that the fans at the Apollo would love my act. He later convinced me to take a shot at it, so I headed to New York to try out for the show.

When I arrived in the Big Apple I made my way to a club called *Stand-Up New York* where they held the Apollo Show auditions. I killed my set and was booked immediately for the show. Not only was I booked, but the producers loved my act so much that they decided to book me as one of the featured guests. I didn't have to worry about being a part of the amateur night and run the risk of getting booed in front of millions of viewers. For the first time in my life my name would be in lights and I would have an opportunity to showcase my talents in front of a nationally televised audience. I was beyond excited.

Over the following few weeks I practiced nonstop and got myself ready for the appearance. I never doubted for a second that I would grace the world famous Apollo stage and dazzle the Harlem crowd. I was always a very cocky performer and I was never afraid of the bright lights. I had played this scenario out in my mind over a thousand times. I imagined the feeling of emerging from beyond the curtains and coming out on stage to perform my act. I fantasized about the cheers and praises. I had heard about a number of performers that suffered from stage fright, but fear was never a problem for me. I was ready to show the world what a little black boy from Palmer Park, Maryland could do with a lot of hard work and determination.

The night of the Apollo taping was an amazing experience for me. There were three other featured acts that evening. Because this was my first major television appearance, a lot of people expected me to be nervous about my performance. I was far from nervous. As my timeslot slowly approached I couldn't help but think about how many talented people performed at the Apollo Theater. I thought back to all the famous feet that graced the stage. It was now my turn to follow in the footsteps of the greats like Michael Jackson, The Supremes, Aretha Franklin, Elton Jon, and so many more. I used there legacies as motivation.

Once Sinbad introduced me to the audience my rollercoaster ride began. As always, I brought the highest energy possible to the stage. The Apollo crowd loved every second of my show. All of my jokes and bits were spot on. As my set continued to flow, my jokes became funnier and the crowd laughed and cheered. Sinbad was absolutely correct about the Apollo crowd. The people loved my show. I had survived one of the toughest stages in America and my accomplishment didn't go unnoticed.

A few weeks later I was flipping through the Sunday newspaper and I scanned through the TV Guide. I searched for the Apollo Show listing and a huge smile came to my face. It was the first time I saw my name in print in the newspaper.

SHOWTIME AT THE APOLLO – Saturday 11:30pm with
Special Guest: Peabo Bryson, Regina Bell,
Kevin Lee & Bill Bellamy

It was an amazing feeling to see my name in the paper as one of the headliners of a nationally televised show. I cut out the TV Guide clipping and I still have it today. The exposure did wonders for my career and I couldn't thank Sinbad enough for convincing me to audition for the show.

Ever since I was a teenager and performing magic at birthday parties, every set has taught me lessons that I used to become a better performer. No matter how good my show was I always felt like I could make it better, bigger and funnier. I never lacked confidence in my skills and I always felt like I could entertain any crowd. Killing the Apollo crowd only boosted my ego and inspired me to push my career forward.

On the night that NBC aired the Apollo episode I sat and watched the entire show. It was a major feat to make it to television and I wanted to enjoy the full experience. I took mental notes on my performance and I paid specific attention to my set and how the audience received it. I was ecstatic about the airing, but something didn't sit right with me. I recorded the show and watched it a dozen more times before I realized what it was that was bothering me.

During the taping of the show I remember killing my set. I stood tall in front of the Apollo crowd and had a flawless performance. At the end of my act I walked off the stage to a huge round of applause. Next up was Regina Belle. She had an amazing show as well. After the R&B set was over it was time for Bill Bellamy. He was also a rising comedian who was quickly gaining notoriety in the industry. At the end of Bill's set he received a huge standing ovation from the Apollo crowd. His audience response compared to mine was very confusing to me. I thought I had a magnificent set, yet I didn't receive a standing ovation from the audience. That puzzled me for a very long time.

Stand-Up Comedy is a very competitive field. Every performer wants to conquer their audience and be the best on any given night. I knew Bill Bellamy was a rising comedic talent and he had a very good set. But it wasn't better than mine. I recorded the show on a VHS tape and probably wore out my remote control with the amount of times I re-winded the episode and analyzed the footage. I paid specific attention to the segments that featured my set and featured Bill's set. I counted the amount of laughs and the amount of applauses that we both received that evening. It was like a boxing match. I tracked the amount of hits connected and points scored by the both of us. By the end of the show I came out on top. I received more laughs and claps during my set. But the question still haunted me. *Why did Bill Bellamy get a standing ovation and I didn't receive one from the Apollo crowd?*

The question swirled in my thoughts for weeks, months and even years. For a long time I couldn't understand why our receptions were so different. I tried to make sense of it but I just couldn't wrap my brain around it. The answer came to me one day when I was replaying the show in my mind. It dawned on me that I had experienced a harsh reality that black audiences back then were not used to a black guy doing magic, juggling and comedy. My set has always been groundbreaking and new to all types of audiences. When people sat down in their chairs to watch a performance, the last thing they expected to see was an African-American man mixing comedy and magic on stage. I had to accept the fact that some crowds were not going to understand my act.

Bill Bellamy has always been a funny comedian. His set on the Apollo Show resonated more with the audience because he did the jokes that they could relate to. He performed bits about "spinning the bottle" when we were kids and other childhood memories that any African American could feel deep in their core. My set may have been funnier to the audience but it was also brand new to them. They had never seen a black guy juggling bowling balls and performing magic tricks that made them laugh. They loved it and cheered me on, but it was also something that they had never seen before. Back in the early 90s, and even up to this day, I have been the most successful African-American Comedian/Magician. Most audiences have no reference point for me. It took a while but I had to accept the fact that I was, and I still am, a pioneer for my brand of comedy.

As my career expanded to more television shows, the name Kevin Lee buzzed throughout the industry and I started to gain more exposure throughout the urban market. The peculiar experience I had at the Apollo Theater would not be the last. It would only take a few months before I found myself introducing my innovative performance style to an even larger African-American audience.

Chapter 11

Def Comedy Jam

A few months before I auditioned for the Apollo Show I was approached by a talent manager named Vern Golf. She was based in the Washington, D.C. area. Vern was one of the most connected African-American women in the music industry. When I opened for Phyllis Hyman at the Carter Barron Amphitheater in Washington, D.C., Vern Golf was in attendance. She loved my set and proposed that she represent me. She was also managing R&B singer Tony Terry who was also from the area. Vern knew little about the comedy world, but she believed in my show. She said that I had a unique act and that she could elevate my exposure and make me a star. I liked the sound of her pitch and decided to sign a contract with her. It turned out to be one of the best decisions I made for my career.

When it was time for me to tape the Apollo Show Vern Golf was right by my side. She was my first professional manager so she did everything she could to help my career. Vern introduced me to a lot of people and gave me some valuable information about the industry. When she learned that I would be on the Apollo Show she didn't hesitate to come out and support me. Backstage, during the taping, Vern ran into a good friend of hers by the name of Bob Sumner. He was working for Def Jam Records and managing Bill Bellamy at the time. Vern introduced me to Bob. When it was time for me to head out on stage, Bob got a chance to see my act and he was very impressed.

About a year later HBO and Russell Simmons partnered to produce a risky new show called *Def Comedy Jam*. It would feature a host of African-American comics that were buzzing throughout the comedy circuit. Russell Simmons hired Bob Sumner to be the talent coordinator for the show. Bob remembered me from my performance at the Apollo Theater , contacted Vern Golf, and they worked out the deal for me to be one of the acts for the first season. I was performing in North Carolina when I got the call from Vern that I would be performing on *Def Comedy Jam*. I didn't know a lot about the show at the time but I knew it would be a great opportunity. It was HBO.

Def Comedy Jam was a groundbreaking show. A lot of careers were jumpstarted from a simple five minute set. Comedians like Bernie Mac, Bill Bellamy, Chris Tucker and Eddie Griffin became huge stars. Even the guys from the show who didn't become household names benefited both financially and professionally. The exposure was amazing. *Def Comedy Jam* was a comedy show that aired on midnight on the largest cable channel on the planet. Everyone was watching the show back then. After my episode aired I began to get recognized everywhere I went. It didn't matter if I was in the United States or out of the country. While on tour with Chris Tucker, Bill Hill and Kevin Anthony, I was recognized by a group of white guys at an airport in Bermuda. The fan love was crazy.

Another time I opened for a rock group called Reo Speedwagon in Hagerstown, Maryland. While we were in the basement of the venue I was recognized by most of the band members in the greenroom. They told me that they had just watched me on *Def Comedy Jam* and really enjoyed my set. Every time someone recognized me from the show I learned more and more of just how popular the show became. I couldn't shop in the mall without being recognized. I would go into P.G. Plaza and Landover Mall near my hometown and people knew who I was.

"That's the guy coming through the window frame." They would yell.

"That's the comedian with the Band Aids on his arm." Someone else would shout out.

Some people didn't know my name but they knew my act. It felt good that people appreciated my performance. For the first time I was being recognized by my people, and that was refreshing. My popularity among African-Americans was skyrocketing. I remember one time I was Christmas shopping in a mall in North Carolina. I overheard a mother and her daughter arguing about me. They were trying to figure out if I was Kevin Lee from *Def Comedy Jam*. "That's him. I'm telling you. That is him." The daughter chuckled. "That's not him." Her mother responded as she looked around. Being recognized when I was out in public was a cool experience. It was a special time for me. One day I was out with my mother shopping, and a group of people recognized me from the show. It was a good feeling to be recognized in public with my mother around. I was happy that she got a chance to see that her son was working hard.

Being on the show also gave way to lot of tour dates. I was tapped to participate in the official *Def Comedy Jam Tour*. We performed nationwide and sometimes out of the country with *Def Jam*. I made a lot of money working those tour dates. Because of the popularity of the show, I was signed by a large booking agency in New York that specialized in booking college shows. They paid me top dollar to perform at several colleges and universities.

I wanted to show off my success, so I bought something brand new. I bought a sports car and started to raise my profile. One day I was performing in Connecticut and I stopped by my agent's house in Bayside, New York. I pulled up to his immaculate home in my fancy red sports car. When I got out the car my agent looked at me with a blank stare.

"What the hell is that?" My agent asked.

"It's my ride." I proudly responded.

"Why are you riding around in that car?" My agent shook his head. "I make ten times more money than you and look at my house. And look at my car."

My agent showed me his car and it was an old beat up car that was about twenty years old. However, my agent's house was amazing. I immediately picked up on the lesson. It was a money lesson that I had never learned from my family. My agent went on to tell me to get rid of the sports car and save my money so that I could be financially secure. It was a great business tip.

As I continued to get booked around the country I noticed that a lot of comedy clubs started doing *Def Comedy Jam Nights*. Instead of booking the urban comics on the hottest nights of the week, a lot of the clubs began to create nights for us. They hired the urban comics in an effort to attract the urban audiences. The agents and club owners segregated the industry. Black comics like me who were accustomed to working the mainstream nights were now forced to work solely on the Def Comedy Jam nights. I was now asked to do Sunday or Wednesday night performances. They removed me from the Friday and Saturday nights where I had performed for years before the HBO show. Agents started to refer to me as a *"Def Jam* Act" which was code word for "black comic." They told me that I could no longer work the white audiences because I was now associated with *Def Comedy Jam*.

The segregation of the industry went on for some time. I found myself working a lot of *Def Comedy Jam* nights and becoming more popular with urban audiences across the country. Those dates were lucrative for me as more mainstream clubs began to invite more black comics to their venues to attract the urban dollar.

The agents and club owners were not the only people who recognized the growing popularity of black comedians. A few years after the debut of *Def Comedy Jam*, BET decided it was time to get in on the action. They developed their own brand of urban stand-up comedy and named it *BET's Comic View*. The show would air exclusively on the black-owned network and feature a cast of urban comics. Most of the *Def Jam* acts that appeared on HBO were hired by BET to help build the popularity of their version. I performed on *BET's Comic View* four times. The audiences loved my act every time I graced the stage.

Once I worked for *BET's Comic View* I noticed a lot of differences with the production. Russell Simmons and his *Def Jam* team treated the comedians and the hosts like stars. They made sure everything was first class when it came to the production of the show. BET was not as generous. Russell Simmons raised the bar very high. The production was very professional. *Def Jam* flew me up from Washington, D.C. to New York and picked me up from the airport in a fancy Town Car. I stayed in a plush hotel in New York City near the theater where they filmed the show.

BET's Comic View was a totally different experience for me. The appearance fee to perform on the show was substantially lower than the average rate for a cable network like BET. Not only was the pay lower, but I was never offered a hotel by the network for any of the appearances. Most comedians were responsible for their travel and lodging during the taping of the shows. I remember getting booked to perform on *Comic View* for a third time and they were taping the episode in New Orleans, Louisiana. I decided to drive down to the taping because I was a comedian on a budget. I performed in front of a live audience and killed the show. Everyone loved it. For those fans that applauded my set, they had no idea that I would be sleeping in a dark parking lot later that evening. BET didn't pay for lodging and by the time I got my check from the network it was too late to rent a hotel.

Being on *BET's Comic View* helped to keep my name buzzing. However, it was far from a financial gain and most comics were not happy about their pay rate. One of the first hosts of the cable show was D.L. Hughley. He was always a quick-witted comic and was never one to bite his tongue. He always spoke his mind and his raw stage act quickly became popular amongst the urban audiences. After a brief stint on the comedy show, D.L. Hughley publicly bashed BET Networks for underpaying its comedians. D.L. accused the executives of using the comics and unfairly duping them out of their fair pay. The going rate for a comparable show on a competing network was $1,000 per episode. BET paid its comics only $100 per episode to tape *Comic View*. The difference of pay was staggering. After D.L.'s accusations reached the newspapers and magazines, the executives at BET decided to make a change. They began to pay all the comedians $1,000 per episode. However, D.L. Hughley never returned to host Comic View after the incident and he has only made a few rare appearances on the network.

The first installments of *Def Comedy Jam* lasted five years. The show's popularity started to die down towards the late 1990's as other comedy shows started popping up on different networks. Due to *Def Comedy Jam's* lack of success during the later years, a lot of the mainstream comedy clubs removed the *Def Jam* nights from their weekly lineups. A lot of the urban comics who made a living doing those club nights were now left to find other ways to survive in this ultra-competitive business.

The transition back to the mainstream comedy nights came very easy for me. I had already built a great network of agents and venues who quickly booked me to perform for their mainstream crowds. Comics who were not versatile and lacked the material to appeal to a mainstream audience eventually moved along and faded away. The comics who refused to die found other ways to capitalize on the popularity of *Def Comedy Jam*. A lot of comics began to rent out their own venues and put together their own shows. Comics like Sommore and Earthquake still make millions of dollars per year on their tours, and they are not considered to be mainstream comics but they are very successful all the same.

The *Def Comedy Jam* phenomenon was a necessary explosion that helped comics like myself expand their brand. The show enticed thousands of club-goers to come out to comedy shows and support the art like never before. The popularity of the show gave us all a platform to grow and express ourselves. Some of the comedians and hosts went on to star in blockbuster movies and Emmy-award winning shows. Dozens of comics are still working today and thriving. What Russell Simmons and Bob Sumner created could never be duplicated. I'll always be grateful for that amazing experience.

Chapter 12

Hookers, Groupies, Playboy Models and Porn Stars

Sex, Drugs and Rock & Roll go together like red, white and blue on the American Flag. In the world of entertainment you can replace the phrase Rock & Roll and get the same result. Sex, Drugs and Sports. Sex, Drugs and Hip-Hop. And in my case it would be Sex, Drugs and Magic. All public figures, no matter their chosen profession, have to deal with men and women lurking in the crowds who are yearning to get next to them. Sex and drugs are a constant in the entertainment business due to these types of overzealous fans. Groupies are addicted to celebrities and seem to sprout up like weeds once you acquire a little bit of fame; and just like weeds, sometimes they get out of control.

The average person will never understand the lengths that a groupie will go to in order to attract an entertainer. It is amazing on several different levels. I've never understood the mindset of a groupie. Then again, I've never asked anyone, *why are you a groupie*? One thing is for sure; they do exist all over the world. I have to admit that I've had my share of groupies. Just like most entertainers, I've taken advantage of the fact that I'm a performer. It's flattering to have a total stranger willing to do anything to be in your presence. I've had women come back to my hotel room without the slightest effort on my part. To be honest, it has happened on more occasions than I can even remember.

I've had encounters with many different types of women all over the world. I remember women of all races, ages, sizes and income brackets. They come plentiful and easily when you are a performer;

109

there's no doubt about it…you get the women. I think every young man in the business—every straight man that is—tries hard to succeed because he knows about the spoils of winning in the entertainment business. When you become rich and famous the women are not far behind. I know a lot of men who got into the business just for the women. At some level deep inside of them they do it all for the pretty women…and the ugly ones, too.

In the past, I've had women come back to my hotel room after a show on several occasions. Each experience was different in its own right. I performed at a comedy club once in Minnesota. Like most of my shows I killed that evening. I met a beautiful young woman and she agreed to come back to my hotel room. I don't remember much about her outside of the fact that she was a Caucasian woman with really large breasts. Things moved rather quickly once we entered the hotel room. Before we got ready to have sex, I went to the bathroom to take a shower. When I returned to the bedroom, the young woman was spread out nude on my bed. There were three lines of cocaine sprinkled on her tits.

"Help yourself," the woman whispered with a sexy grin.

I thought for a moment as I looked at her. I have always been a healthy guy and never wanted to put my body at risk of getting addicted to drugs. The woman was very attractive. But she was not worth the problems that would come with snorting the cocaine.

I shook my head and said the first thing that came to my mind. "No thanks. I don't do drugs."

The look on her face said it all. My decision not to do drugs ruined the moment. She was turned off by the fact that I didn't want to go *Scarface* on her breasts. The tension in the room began to thicken as we both fell silent. I wasn't a drug addict or drug user and I refused to start on her breasts. Sniffing cocaine was just something that I managed not to have in my life, and I wasn't going to include it that night. We ended up sitting in bed most of the night and just talking. The woman stayed in my room until early the next morning, then she got dressed and left. Nothing happened. I laugh sometimes with my friends when I tell them the story about that night. It always cracks me up how I was able to resist the cocaine-titties in Minnesota.

There has been many times like that. I remember being at Virginia Tech and a young girl brought me back to her dorm room. It was almost the same scenario. Another female offering me sex and drugs. When I got in the young lady's room, she brought out a large bong. I'm listed on my driver's license as six-feet and one inch tall and I believe the bong was just as tall as I was. I had never seen a bong that large before. I watched her as she emptied a thick bag a weed in the bong. She invited her girlfriend to join us in her room.

At this point I'm in a college dorm room with two young hot women and they are ready to get high with me and have some fun. The first girl hit the bong and took a long pull. I could tell it was some good weed because a smile came to her face. She handed the bong to her girlfriend. Both of the girls gave me a sexy look and started to take off some of their clothes. They didn't know much about me, but there I was, lying in bed with them. They were hot for me and wanting to jump my bones just because I was a comedian that made them laugh at the show earlier.

The girl who had invited me to the room actually pulled out some pictures. She smiled and laughed as she showed them to me.

"I got high with Ice Cube and Dr. Dre before." The girl chuckled. The weed was definitely getting to her.

She showed me pictures of her and a group of friends hanging with different celebrities that visited their school. Some photos were taken backstage of the concerts and some of them were taken at the campus parties. Her claim to fame was taking photos with dozens of celebrities who got high with her. She was a very pretty girl. She was in college and seemed to have a lot going for herself. She wasn't the typical groupie material. But I learned that day that educated girls could be groupies, too.

After the girls took me down memory lane with their photos they were ready to have some real fun. The three of us started kissing and undressing each other. Before things could get too hot, they started smoking the bong again. Of course, they passed it to me. And with me being Mr. Drug-Free Guy, I couldn't help but respond honestly.

"Oh, I don't do drugs," I said as I shook my head.

"Awh come on…take a hit," one of the girls egged me on.

I looked at the sexy hot girls again and decided to give in. I didn't want to ruin my chance at a spontaneous threesome that evening. I grabbed the bong from the girl's hand and took a hit. I did my best Bill Clinton impression and I didn't inhale. I pretended like I was smoking on the bong but I was faking it. I'm a magician; I can fake these things, right? Wrong!

I mistakenly took a long pull of the bong and a thick cloud of smoke attacked my virgin lungs. I started coughing uncontrollably as my body tried to recover from the smoldering invasion. The girls started laughing at me. I could only imagine what they were thinking as I coughed up all of the coolness out of my superstar persona. I had never smoked weed before and had no idea what I was doing. The young girls could see that I was a novice and all of my coughing ruined the mood. There were no drug-filled sex-capades that evening. The night ended with me leaving the sexy girls alone with their bong. I never got to take a photo with them to add to their collection.

My lack of drug use has costs me numerous fun nights while I was on the road back then. I always put my health and my life before any peer pressure that was thrown in my direction. I could never bring myself to do anything that would jeopardize my career. There was no way I would put myself in a position to lose everything that I had worked so hard to gain.

In my travels I have learned a few things about groupies. I learned that not all groupies are drug users and not all groupies are single. I have been lucky enough to meet drug-free hot women and I have also met some women who were married. Sometimes the fascination of being with an entertainer is so great that women will break their sacred vows for one night of excitement.

One evening after I finished a comedy show in Alexandria, Virginia I was approached by a woman who had just finished watching my set. I was staying on the sixth floor of the Holiday Inn and the woman followed me into the elevator. As the doors closed the woman moved closer and pressed up against me. We were alone and the woman seized the opportunity to tell me about a fantasy she had harbored for years. She told me that she had never been with a black man. Oddly enough the woman told me she was married and she showed me pictures of her husband and kids. The woman went on to explain that she was a dentist in the Boston area and she was traveling on business. She didn't hesitate to tell me how badly she wanted to be with a black man. She was very attractive and I made up my mind immediately that I was going to help her act out her fantasy.

As the elevator reached my floor my phone started ringing. I wanted to ignore the call and take the woman back to my room but the person continued to redial my number. I looked down to the phone and realized that it was my brother Henry calling. He didn't sound good when I picked up the line and he told me that he needed my help. He was dealing with a lot of drug issues at that time so I knew I had to help him. I turned to the woman with a look of disappointment. I told her that I had to leave the hotel and that her fantasy had to wait for another black man to come long. My brother was in trouble and for as long as I could remember, my family always came first. The dentist from Boston was not the last married woman to offer herself up to me.

During my earlier days as a traveling comic I performed in many towns that people have never heard of. I have been to various parts of the country where I was the only black person for miles at a time. I remember performing in a small town in Western Pennsylvania. The town was deep in the mountains. I was booked to perform at an Elk's Lodge for about one hundred people. Once I arrived to the area I could tell that I was in a very *different* part of America. When I got near the center of town I stopped at a gas station to fill up. The gas attendant recognized me and told me that he knew I was in town to perform that evening. As we talked I could tell that he had never spoken to a black man in his life. I knew I was in for an interesting trip.

Later that evening my show was a success. The people who came out to see me really had a good time and they enjoyed my set. After the stage performance I hung out with the fans and took a few pictures. One man came up to me and told me how funny I was. He explained to me that he and his wife would love for me to come back to their house for drinks. He told me that they had a really nice house with a hot tub. I was young and didn't think anything of his invite, so I agreed to go over their house and hang out with them.

The couple was very nice. Everything seemed normal at first. After a few drinks the couple got into their hot tub and invited me to join them. I got undressed and got inside the tub. It didn't take long for me to find out the real reason why I was invited over to their place. The man leaned over to me and told me that he and his wife had a fantasy. He told me that he wanted me to sleep with his wife while he watched us. The request shocked me. I had heard of a lot of kinky things before but nothing like that. I was also young and adventurous so the offer intrigued me. That night I put my fears aside and played out the fantasy with them. That night in the mountains was not the last time that I got approached by a married couple that was looking for some kinky fun.

Throughout my travels I have had a lot of wild and crazy sex. I've been with a lot of women and I've done my share of dirt in big and small towns alike. I sometimes jokingly referred to myself as an International Lover because I've slept with women from all over the world. There were women in Japan, women in Korea, women in Italy, women in Spain, women in London, women in Germany, women in Guam—believe it or not, women in Iceland, women in Sweden…and of course, women from all over the United States. I never discriminated when it came to lovers.

I can honestly say that I have done my business everywhere. It is hard not to brag about my dealings because I was a man on a mission. I had various reasons why I felt the need to be very promiscuous and around women all the time. It was like sex just came with the life of being a traveling comedian. I would have never met the women that

I've slept with if I wasn't an entertainer. I never considered myself to be an unattractive guy or lacking in good traits, but I know a lot of the women that I fooled around with did these things because of my chosen profession.

One of the wildest sexual encounters that I can remember happened in a grocery store in Greenbelt, Maryland. A few days prior I had performed there at a location called *The Comedy Connection*. I was shopping in a Safeway Food Market and while walking down aisle #3 I was approached by a sexy woman. I didn't recognize her at all but she clearly recognized me. She told me that she had seen my show at the comedy club and she loved looking at me on stage. We talked for a few minutes in the aisle before things turned hot. The woman was very aggressive as she moved closer to me. Before I could say another word she unzipped my pants and pulled out my manhood right there in the grocery store. She had no fear of getting caught.

The woman performed oral sex on me right there in the middle of the store. This was years before cell phone cameras and high tech store surveillance. The weirdest thing about that situation was the fact that I didn't stop her. I got lost in the moment and I just let it happen. It was a miracle that we didn't get caught. No one ever stopped us. The excitement of risking arrest for public indecency just added to the thrill. I never saw the woman again after that day in the Greenbelt Safeway. She wasn't interested in exchanging numbers with me. She just wanted to share a wild moment with an entertainer. Nothing more. It was definitely one of the crazier moments in my life.

Those wild days of my life didn't stop when I left the country. My first time with a hooker was in Seoul, Korea back in the late 80s. It was during the Miller Comedy Tour. One of the first things I learned soon after I touched down in Korea was the fact that prostitution was legal there. After landing at the airport we were picked up and taken to our hotel. We were staying in a very nice Hyatt Regency. Everyone in the hotel seemed to know that we were coming. They all knew that we were from America and they treated us very well. The bellman carried my luggage to my room and told me that I would have a good time in Korea. I made sure to tip him before he left the room. A few minutes later I heard a knock on the door. I thought it was the bellman returning to speak with me, but I was surprised when I opened the door and laid my eyes on an attractive Korean woman.

"Mr. Lee, I am here to serve the American," she said in a sexy voice.

And serve me she did. The prostitute knew my name and I immediately picked up on the game. The вellman/pimp sent the girl to my room immediately after he returned down to the lobby. He made sure I had an enjoyable stay, and that was not the last time I would pay for a hooker in Korea.

When I returned from the Miller Comedy Tour and started traveling more around the United States, it seemed that my caliber of women began to elevate. One weekend I was booked to perform a series of comedy shows in Dade County in Miami, Florida. The name of the club was *Uncle Funnies*. This was a few years after my overseas trip and just after my days on *Def Comedy Jam*. My friend and I stayed at the Holiday Inn which was right next to the Joe Robbie Stadium where the Miami Dolphins played. While we were staying at the Holiday Inn, we went to a strip club during the day to kill time before the evening shows. On this particular day we noticed that there was a book signing going on inside of the strip club.

The signing was for a tall, 6'2", blond beauty. She was an absolutely gorgeous woman. She was a recent Playboy centerfold model. There was a long line of people there waiting to get an autographed copy of her feature Playboy magazine centerfold. Even though she was very beautiful, I didn't stand in the line to get an autograph. I went over to the bar instead to order a soda and a salad. I've always been a health food nut and even in the strip clubs I would find something healthy to eat.

A few minutes later I noticed that the Playboy model was getting ready to shut her event down. As she packed up for the day we made eye contact. There were nearly seventy men hovering around her during the signing and after we made eye contact it was like none of them existed. That eye contact led to a brief conversation and then led to us spending the entire weekend at the Holiday Inn in Dade County.

Inviting her back to my room caused a small problem. My friend was working with me in the area and we had a hotel room together. However, my new 6' 2" blond roommate-for-the-weekend forced him to make other arrangements. He was a young comic I hired to come on the road with me so he understood that I needed the room. He ended up staying in the laundry room of the Holiday Inn because he couldn't afford to rent an extra room. He left with a blanket and pillow and crashed in the basement all weekend.

My weekend was much different. I hung out with the Playboy Model during my entire stay and we had a ball together. She was extremely outgoing and of course she was well endowed. When we hung out everyone that saw us together was envious. I found out later that the model was married to a military guy who was stationed in Germany. Our weekend fling lasted only for those few short days but I never forgot her. Not many people can say that they spent the weekend with a Playboy Model.

Although I had some wild times in my life, some of my situations turned out to be disasters. Being an entertainer doesn't give you a lot of time to get to know the opposite sex before things turn physical. I've had dozens of one-night stands and very short relationships in my life. Some of them were full of excitement and thrills, and some of them were simply mistakes in judgment that could have cost me my life.

During my days at the *Comedy Café* in Washington, D.C. I used to frequent a strip club named *Archibald's* that was located just above the comedy club, in the same building. The owner gave strict orders to the comedians that we were not to talk or date any of the strippers from the club. He was very serious about his rules and very overprotective of his dancers. I knew about his orders but like everything else in my life, there was no fun in following the rules.

A few months later I found myself dating one of the sexiest

strippers from the club. She was a fierce girl and she had all the looks to compliment her outgoing nature. We were able to keep our relationship a secret for nearly a year. We moved in together and had a lot of fun. Unfortunately the relationship didn't last long. She started to show me another side of her and I didn't like it. She began to threaten me a lot. An ugly side of her started to surface and every day I grew nervous. After the second time she tried to stab me, I decided it was time to get out of that relationship and leave her crazy ass for good.

The world of entertainment could be wild at times. I had a lot of fun as an emerging comic. Traveling around the world and meeting new people from different cultures was simply an amazing joy ride. I learned a lot about the women I was with. I learned a lot about the world. And most importantly I learned a lot about myself. As I grew more mature and started to slow down, I began to realize why I was so promiscuous and hell-bent on sleeping with any woman I could find. The answer came to me in an unexpected rush. I had to face a harsh reality that was buried deep within my childhood.

▲

Old street performing photo.

Early promo shots for
Comedian /Magician Kevin Lee ▶

First of many write-ups in
Washingtonian Magazine

▼

Way back in the day
with Jamie Foxx

▼

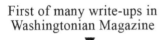

A Somber Panel Laughs at Twinkies and a

Washingtonian Magazine

Kevin Lee and
The Legendary Jacksons

Backstage with Gladys Knight
and my mother Catherine

▼ 1992 Def Comedy Jam
Performance

▼Bill Cosby and Kevin Lee

▼ BETs Comic View
taping live in New Orleans

▼ Comedy star Fazion Love
and Kevin Lee in Mami Fl.

Kevin Lee and Legendary Comedian
George Wallace

Arriving in Los Angeles
with my daughter Solina

▼Kevin Lee & Comedian Luenell

▼ On the set of Season 9
of NBC's Last Comic Standing

▼ On the set of one of the many
news channels in the country

Visiting a Military Hospital
1987 Overseas Comedy Tour

Filming a beer commercial
in Japan

Legendary Radio and TV Star
▼ Donnie Simpson and Kevin Lee

Official Tour Poster ▼
Gladys Knight & Kevin Lee

R&B singer Eric Benet
▼ and Kevin Lee in Jamaica

Radio Interview Pittsburg, PA

Kevin Lee and Actress
Pam Grier

My best friend in the comedy game
The Legendary Fat Doctor

Great comedian and longtime
▼ buddy Tommy Davidson

Filming "Last Comic Standing"
▼ Segment on Venice Beach, CA

Street Performing on The National
▼ Mall in Washington, DC

Solina and I joking around in one of our 1-Bedroom Apartments

Teaching my young daughter Karate and Self Defense

Signing autographs in Bahrain
▼ in the Middle East

▼My suitcase filled with money after a day of street performing

Dropping Solina off for her
▼ first day of College

Celebrating My 50th Birthday
with My Father

At The MGM With The Living
Legend David Copperfield

▼　　Wanda Sykes and I
performing on tour in Las Vegas

My cousin Dennis Jeter
and I and our magic show.
▼　　Sky's the limit.

▼　　My Brother Heny and I

▼ Celebrating Christmas with my
sister Bridgette & my brother Henry

Me and my Beautiful Mom

Patricia and I.
Behind every good man is a
wonderful woman.

The last gift that my sister
Dawn gave to me
▼ two weeks before she died.

My sister Dawn Brooks
▼ (Rest In Peace)

Chapter 13

My Pride and Joy

After appearing on HBO's *Def Comedy Jam* and numerous episodes of BET's *Comic View*, I often referred to myself as a mini-celebrity. A simple trip to the mall or to a restaurant would turn into an elaborate guessing-game for my fans. It's difficult for me to recall all the people who tried to guess my name or asked me why I looked familiar to them. Hundreds of people knew my act and sometimes they knew who I was. It was always fun to interact with my fans and watch them laughing at my stand-up routine. Some of my fans were a lot of fun and some fans were downright clueless.

One Saturday evening I was standing outside of a Baltimore Hotel. I had just finished performing at a comedy show and decided to hang out in front of the hotel and enjoy the scene. A few minutes later an older Caucasian woman approached me. She appeared to be in her mid-50s. The woman stared at me for a moment and then a large smile came to her face.

"Oh my God, I just love your show." The woman continued to smile.

I nodded my head and returned the smile.

"Oh wow," I responded. "I'm happy to hear that you love my show. Thank you."

"You are quite welcome," the woman said with excitement. "My children watch you all the time."

I immediately grew confused. I gave the woman a strange look. I couldn't recall any children watching my show.

"I need to get your autograph," the woman said and scrambled to find a pen. "My kids are not going to believe this. They watch you all the time on *The Fresh Prince of Bel-Air.*"

At that moment I had to make a decision. It was the first time I was asked to sign an autograph, but the request was bittersweet. Part of me was disappointed that I was mistaken for Will Smith but also a part of me found the encounter to be comical. I didn't want to break this sweet woman's heart, so I asked to borrow her pen. Just as the woman requested I signed Will's name on a piece of paper. I didn't have the heart to tell the woman I wasn't *The Fresh Prince.*

Those early days of being on television were filled with a lot of memorable encounters. Being stopped by fans and bumping into old friends seemed to be a daily routine when I ventured out in public. I didn't mind the fanfare. I was flattered by the attention I received. Some people were very nice and meeting me simply made their day. However, on a few occasions I would meet people who were not so thrilled to see me. I remember having a strange exchange with a man who recognized me from television. I was on the street and I needed to make a call. This was back in the days before mobile phones. If you were on the move and needed to make a call, you had to use a public phone. On this particular day I found myself in that very position. I needed to make a quick call. A man walked by me just as I picked up the receiver on the public phone.

"Hey, aren't you the comedian from *Def Comedy Jam*?" The man asked as he stared at my face. "What the hell are you doing on a pay phone?"

The question was strange, and the man didn't stick around for an answer. He was clearly the type of person that was clueless about how show business works. When people see you on television they believe that you have officially made it. I guess the guy assumed that I was a millionaire at the time and had no use for public phones. He was clearly wrong.

Despite my television appearances I was still building my career. Outside of the initial appearance fees I received from HBO and BET, all of my income was coming from my tour dates and gigs at the comedy clubs. I was far from a millionaire, but I was doing well for myself. When the money started rolling in I purchased anything that would make me look good. I bought expensive clothes and shoes and even made sure I bought a fancy car. When people seen me in public I wanted to look like a star. I have always been a big believer in the concept of "*fake it 'til you make it.*" I never wanted people to think that I was unsuccessful.

One year around Christmas time I was helping my family, who were still living in Maryland. My stepfather, Mr. Sheldon, was always the consummate businessman. He would take over a large piece of property and sell Christmas trees every year. If I wasn't booked for a show I would help my brother Henry run the lot while Mr. Sheldon collected the money and handled other business. One day while we were working, my brother asked me to run to the store for him. I didn't mind at all. I headed to the store and grabbed a few items. When I returned to Mr. Sheldon's lot I noticed that my brother Henry was speaking with a person I hadn't seen in over fifteen years.

A rush of raw emotions ran through me when I looked at the man's face. I felt the pent-up rage that was buried for over a decade as it began to resurface. Old feelings of shame and betrayal filled my mind. I told myself that if I ever saw this son-a-bitch again that I would make him pay for all the pain he caused me. Over the years I had physically trained to kick his ass, and the thought of punishing him crossed my mind. I never thought in a million years that I would see my stepbrother again. But there he was. The boy who molested me and repeatedly raped me in California was finally within striking distance.

My brother Henry was unaware of the dark history that I shared with my stepbrother. Henry didn't know about the painful nights I experienced during that summer in California. Every sick memory came to my mind as I looked my abuser in the eyes. I could tell that he was afraid of me. His appearance was very dirty and he looked as if he had a serious drug problem. His life had clearly spiraled downward toward a tragic conclusion. For many years I fantasized about beating the life out of my stepbrother. I wanted to repay him for the physical, emotional and psychological damage he caused me. But after taking one look at him I knew that I had my revenge. I looked at his pathetic life, then I looked at my life and I knew I had won. Our lives were headed in two opposite directions. I never confronted my stepbrother about the abuse nor did I put my hands on him. We spoke very briefly that afternoon and we went our separate ways. From that day I have never seen my stepbrother again.

It's funny how life will throw you a curveball when you least expect it. Going through the abuse as a child caused me a lot of undeserved pain and guilt. In my early twenties I forced those dark memories to the back of my mind. I used my anger as fuel to motivate me to be a winner. I was running from the pain of my youth so that I could be a successful adult. From state to state, from comedy show to comedy show, it was like I had to prove to myself that I wasn't afraid any more. When I met women out on the road I would make it a mission to sleep with them. I wanted to prove that I was strong and could handle my business. Being abused as a young child made me shy and timid at times but I wanted to change that as an adult. I wanted to be *the man* when it came to the opposite sex. I became a womanizer. I didn't care who got hurt. It was a selfish time in my life that went on for years. There were so many women that came in and out of my life. It became impossible to remember their names and who they were. It is a fact that I would have never met these women if I wasn't an entertainer. Just as I was abused as a child, I abused the privilege of being a popular comedian. The women were like drugs to me. A new city would bring a new woman to have fun with. Some women were easily forgotten. But one chance encounter in Virginia Beach would introduce me to a woman that would change my life forever.

In 1992, my career was being managed by a guy by the name of Pop Thomas. He was a real good guy who worked extremely hard for his clients. He represented a few comedians in the area and he hustled hard to keep us busy with gigs and appearances. After working with him for a few months, Pop Thomas booked me to perform at a comedy event in Virginia Beach. The venue was primarily a nightclub with a live DJ, dancing and drinks the entire night. The club would host comedy shows on Thursdays, and Pop Thomas booked me periodically to headline the shows.

One evening I was standing outside of the venue after one of my shows. I had just finished performing in front of a sold out crowd. Like most evenings back in those days, I would sit outside and mingle with the guests who just finished watching me on stage. Back in those days I was the true definition of an attention addict. I would sit on the hood of my red sports car and wait for people to approach me to tell me how much they loved my show. The attention was intoxicating some nights. I met dozens of women that way. It was an easy way to break the ice.

On this particular evening a young woman caught my eye. She was extremely attractive with a model-like body. She was wearing a short mini skirt that immediately grabbed my attention. She was a light-skinned black woman who reminded me of the actress Lisa Bonet. When we made eye contact I could tell that there was an immediate attraction. The pretty young woman never stopped to speak to me. We smiled at each other as she made her way into the club. On this particular night the venue was transitioning from a comedy night to a dance party. It was clear that the woman was here for the after party and not the comedy show. After a few minutes I couldn't get the woman's face out of my head. Instead of leaving for the night, I decided to go back into the club. I needed to meet this mystery woman.

When I walked back inside I found her at the bar. She was ordering a drink so I decided to join her. I introduced myself. She politely followed by telling me her name was Venus. She didn't see the comedy show that evening and had no clue that I was an emerging comedian. We talked for a good while and we immediately hit it off. Our mutual attraction was undeniable.

After a couple of hours of conversation and drinks, Venus asked me for a ride home. She told me that she had come to the event alone.

I didn't want the night to end so I told her that I was staying at a hotel not too far away. I asked Venus to come hang out with me and she agreed. I had traveled to the area with another comedian and we were roommates for the trip. When Venus and I returned from the party I immediately kicked him out of the hotel room. I wanted to spend the entire evening with my new friend and that is exactly what we did.

The next morning I dropped Venus off at home. We exchange numbers and we managed to stay in touch once I returned to Maryland. Venus and I would see each other when I wasn't on tour or busy with my other women. Sometimes I took the train to the Virginia Beach area, and sometimes Venus traveled north to Maryland. We hung out and had a lot of fun together. We were insanely attracted to one another on a psychical level so we would have sex any chance we could.

During the first few months of our friendship, the distance didn't keep us from communicating. We paged each other quite often and spoke on the phone every week. Venus was big into writing, so she would write a lot of heartfelt letters to me. Some letters were seven to eight pages long. She would tell me how much she missed me and loved me and how our encounters were very special to her. I would write letters back to her and over time the letters helped us stay in touch.

One day I received a letter from Venus that left me in total shock. We had been dating for just over four months and Venus had written to give me some news. She told me that she was pregnant and that I was going to be a father. I was frozen by the words on the page. It was hard for me to believe that I was going to be a dad. I knew that Venus was in a relationship back in Virginia Beach so I was suspicious that someone else could be the father. I was a young single man with multiple women in my circle and I wanted to believe that this was a misunderstanding. I confronted Venus about the news and she told me that she was sure the child was mine.

It took a few days for me to process Venus' letter. I had been running nonstop for a lot of years. My career was filled with comedy nights, international gigs and meeting women all over the world. Being a father was the last thing on my mind. As the days turned to weeks and months I had to come to grips with my new reality. I was going to be a father and it was time for me accept my responsibilities. On August 6th of that year Venus went into labor and gave birth. I received a call from her stepmother, Judy, who revealed the news that Venus had given birth to a healthy baby girl. The news humbled me and I felt a cocktail of emotions. I was nervous, excited and tense. I wanted to see my daughter and asked Venus to bring her to Maryland. Venus agreed and she took the trip up to my apartment about five weeks later. My mother was so excited. She came over with gifts and her camera so she could take plenty of pictures of her grandchild. When Venus arrived with our bundle of joy it was a very proud moment for me. I was finally introduced to my daughter Solina. I instantly fell in love.

Chapter 14

Going Back To Cali

After the birth of my daughter in 1993, my life began to change dramatically. There are no words to describe the feeling of seeing Solina for the first time. She was just a tiny infant but she had a major impact on my life. I couldn't believe that I was a father. It motivated me to do everything I could to make sure Solina was taken care of and had everything she needed. I was living with Fat Doctor, Pop and Chris Paul. a few of my friends and fellow comedians at the time. We were all constantly working, traveling and making our mark in the industry. One of my good friends and roommate Chris Paul was a rapper and comedian. Chris ended up getting a radio gig with the popular *Donny Simpson Show* in Washington, DC that year and he eventually moved out. My best friend Fat Doctor later got his own apartment so I decided to move out as well. I knew things were going to change for me now that Solina was in the picture. I searched for a new place to live and eventually moved into my own apartment in Maryland. I tried to see my daughter as much as I could. Her mother Venus and I didn't have a strong relationship at that point. Between my comedy career and the other women, I continued to live the lifestyle of a player. But that all changed.

One evening I was performing at a comedy club called *Jokes On Us* in Laurel, Maryland. The venue was a popular spot for comedians on the rise and established acts. Martin Lawrence, Tommy Davidson, Monique, Mark Curry and Earthquake were just a few of the notable names that came through to perform at the club. *Jokes On Us* was one of the premiere urban comedy clubs that exclusively featured acts from the black circuit. The club owner was also my manager during those days, so I spent a lot of time at the club.

That particular night I was headlining a show at the venue. I was performing a bit where I asked a young lady to come onto the stage and assist me. After a few moments of scanning the audience, I zeroed in on a strikingly beautiful woman in the front row. I was compelled to bring her up on stage. I performed my signature routine where I blindfolded the woman and juggled knives during the set. The woman was a good sport and we had a lot of fun on stage together. After the bit was over, the woman returned to her seat and the audience gave her a big round of applause.

After the show I headed out to the lobby to meet with my fans. I always take pictures and sign autographs after my shows and that evening was no different. I saw the attractive woman who came on stage. She was with her boyfriend. He was a popular player for the Washington Redskins and she was dating him. She shook my hand and complimented me on the show. We spoke for a few minutes and they left the comedy club. I thought I would never see the woman again.

A few minutes later the woman returned to the club. She told the NFL player that she needed to use the restroom but that was just an excuse to come back alone. She walked up to me and slipped me her phone number. I was surprised by the move but I was happy she came back. I didn't know it at the time but her decision to return to the club would change the course of my life. Her name was Anne, and she eventually became my wife.

After meeting Anne, I decided that I didn't want to be a player any more. I broke it off with all of my other women and put all of my energy into this amazing woman I met at the comedy club. I learned that Anne was a student at the University of Maryland and she was also a live-in nanny for a rich white family in McLean, Virginia. Anne and I immediately hit it off. It didn't take long for her to leave the professional football player and move into my little apartment. I was surprised that Anne left a man who was making millions of dollars to come and live with a comedian who was living paycheck to paycheck. But with Anne, our connection was deeper than just money. We had a wonderful relationship.

The NFL player didn't go away quietly. He would call her all the time and leave her voicemails. When she decided to relocate to Maryland, I helped her move her things out of her basement apartment in McLean, Virginia. Anne played the voicemails from her ex-boyfriend. I could hear him begging and crying for her to return. It never happened. Anne and I started renting a one-bedroom apartment in Laurel, Maryland, and our relationship began to flourish.

Anne had everything I wanted in a woman. She was supportive of my career and we were nuts about each other. Anyone looking at our relationship from the outside could tell that we were madly in love with each other. Our relationship moved fast. After a few months of dating I proposed to Anne. She agreed to take my hand in marriage and become Mrs. Lee. We didn't have a traditional wedding because our families were so far apart from each other. Anne was originally from The Republic of Sri Lanka which is located just off the coast of India. She was adopted when she was just a toddler by a family in Sweden. Anne was raised in Northern Europe before moving to the United States. When we got married, Anne and I traveled to Sweden to be with her family and partake in a ceremony to celebrate our union. It was a very special time.

When we returned to the United States, Anne and I began to build our life together. I added more comedy gigs to my schedule and Anne did everything she could to support me. Now that I was a married man, I was eager to build my family with two very special females in my life; my wife and my daughter. Anne and I traveled to Virginia a number of times to pick up Solina for the weekend. I was still in contact with Solina's mother but she began to go through major issues that affected my daughter. Venus found herself getting arrested and having legal problems in Virginia. After a serious drug-related arrest, Venus was forced to relinquish custody of Solina. My daughter would now be living with Venus' adopted mother, Judy, while she carried out her sentence at a job core program in Virginia.

141

I was not happy to hear that my daughter had become a meal ticket for Judy. Venus' mother received monthly assistance for helping to raise Solina, so Judy was not interested in allowing me to see my daughter. Judy was no fan of Kevin Lee. Instead of picking up my daughter from Venus, I was now forced to deal with Judy directly. Judy and I didn't have the best relationship from the beginning and things grew progressively worse. Judy was very strict when it came time for me to get my daughter for the weekend. If I returned her an hour late Judy would bicker and fuss with me. Judy became impossible to deal with but I never stopped going back and forth to Virginia to see my daughter.

One day my wife and I discussed the possibility of moving to California. I had previously moved to the west coast to further my career but I knew this time would be different. Anne and I sent a promotional tape to a big talent manager by the name of Chuck Harris in California. He got a chance to review my television appearances on *Uptown Comedy Club* and *Def Comedy Jam*. Chuck immediately loved my act and contacted me.

"Kevin, the bit you performed when you sprayed down the microphone on Martin Lawrence is one of the funniest jokes I have ever seen," Chuck said to me. "I have seen a lot of funny comedians after forty years of being in this business. You are going to be a star. I've only been wrong once in my life and that was with my first wife. If you move to Los Angeles I will manage you. I won't manage you from the east coast. You have to be in L.A."

After having the conversation with Chuck Harris I made up my mind. I decided to take the leap of faith and move to the west coast with my new wife. It was a major opportunity to help my career, so Anne and I made preparations for the relocation.

Meanwhile, back in Virginia, Judy heard the news that I was moving to California. She grew nervous and feared that I was planning to take my daughter away from Virginia. She didn't want to lose custody of Solina so Judy stopped allowing me to see my daughter. She never returned any of my calls. Venus was away at the job core program and she was impossible to reach. For nearly a month I tried to see my daughter but I was unsuccessful. Judy went missing on me. My wife and I eventually packed up a U-Haul truck and headed cross-country. We moved to Van Nuys, California and found a nice apartment where we chose to begin our life on the west coast. Once I got settled into our new place, I tried to reach out to Judy once again. I called back to Virginia but the phone number was no longer in service. Judy had severed all lines of communication and I eventually lost total contact with my daughter.

From the moment my wife and I pulled up to the front of our new apartment I could tell that California was going to be a different speed. I was now in a great position to take my career to new heights and I was happy to have Anne right there by my side. It didn't take long for us to get a pleasant introduction to California living. One day my wife and I went to the local Boston Market Restaurant to order dinner. Standing just a few feet away in the same line was my good friend and celebrity Tommy Davidson. I hadn't seen Tommy since working with him in the D.C. area and we were happy to reconnect. My wife Anne was star-struck. She couldn't believe that we were friends. Tommy and I exchanged numbers and he even invited me to a few gigs in the area. Running into Tommy was just the beginning of a long list of chance encounters during my time on the west coast.

Within a few weeks I found myself deep within the comedy scene in Los Angeles. My new manager Chuck Harris was well connected and he was able to open doors for me fairly quickly. I began to do audience warm-ups for a few sitcoms including the hit television show "In The House" which starred LL Cool J and Debbie Allen. My manager also booked me to do dozens of casino and college shows as well. My career started to elevate with each successful gig. The caliber of work was very different from the comedy clubs that were available to me back in Maryland. Every weekend seemed to bring a new opportunity to showcase my act. I started running into familiar faces all over the place. I was confident that it would be just a matter of time before I got my shot at a television show or a movie.

Before I left Maryland I underestimated the competition that was waiting for me on the west coast. I was no longer competing with local comedians for weekly gigs at the comedy clubs back in my home state. I was now competing with A-List celebrities with established names in the game. I wanted to keep up with the people that made it big so I bought a new sports car and made sure that I wore the latest fashions whenever I was out in public. I was a rising star in the area and I wanted to blend in with the big boys. I hung around an endless group of celebrities. I would spend a lot of nights at a club called *The Comedy Store* on Sunset Boulevard in Hollywood. I met a lot of well-known comedians at *The Comedy Store* including the legendary Richard Pryor. In less than a year I was making noise in California and it felt like I was living a dream.

Not long after I moved to California my best friend, The Fat Doctor, contacted me. He had been working with Martin Lawrence for a good while and managed to land a well-paying job as a writer on the hit sitcom *Martin*. When he moved to California he asked if he could live with me and my wife and I agreed. I rented out our second room to him. It was cool to be living with my new wife and my best friend. The Fat Doctor and I hung out a lot. We went to comedy clubs every week together and also hung out when we were back at the apartment. We knew a lot of comedians and most of them would also come by the apartment and hang out with us. On any given night there would be a group of people playing video games, smoking weed and hanging out at my place.

While I was chasing the Hollywood lifestyle and building my career, my wife was experiencing a different side of California. Anne searched for employment every week during those first few months in Van Nuys. Her job search was fruitless. She completed dozens of resumes but all of the well-paying jobs seemed to go to other people. When Anne would visit the temp agencies they would suggest housekeeping work for her. She ended up doing odd jobs and moving from one part-time job to another. My wife soon grew frustrated and her family back in Sweden started to question her decision to marry me. Her adopted parents wanted her to marry a rich man so she would never have to worry about money. They scolded her about being with a man who was living off comedy gigs and inconsistent shows. Her parents were also upset by the fact that she dropped out of college and they blamed me for her decision. Anne's frustrations only grew as my bookings slowed down and our money became tight. We got behind on bills and we eventually were evicted from our nice apartment.

The eviction dealt a major blow to our relationship. I was not making a lot of money and Anne had to become the bread winner for us. The topic of money was a major issue that began to boil over and put a strain on our marriage. As I continued to search for more gigs and increase my income, Anne did everything she could to help my career. She even wrote a letter to Jay Leno who was hosting *The Tonight Show* in Los Angeles at the time. Anne told Jay Leno about my career and that I was an upcoming comedian searching for work. She told him about our struggles and wanted to know if Jay Leno could help. To our surprise Jay Leno called our house. I wasn't home at the time and Jay Leno had to leave a message with my wife. We prayed that Jay Leno would call us back and a few weeks later he did. Jay Leno called us on eviction day. We were served a three-day notice to vacate and Jay Leno called on the day that we were moving our things. When we returned to the apartment to grab our final items we noticed there was a voice message on our machine. It was from the host of *The Tonight Show*. He left us a message but there was no return phone number. Heaven only knows how our lives would have turned out if we were home to answer Jay Leno's call.

Anne and I were in California for nearly two years before things really began to fall apart. Because of my lack of success and my lack of focus on my wife, Anne began to search for attention in other places. The reality of having a struggling career was embarrassing. Being financially incapable of taking care of my wife was frustrating. But all of those misfortunes pale in comparison to the pain of learning that my wife was having an affair on me. I would have never believed in a million years that I would drive Anne into the arms of another man.

When I learned of the affair I was shocked. I immediately fell into a deep depression and our relationship quickly unraveled. It became impossible for me to understand her decision. Anne shattered my heart into a thousand pieces. We were both young and I was unaware that I was neglecting her. Leaving Anne alone at home when I was out at the comedy clubs opened up the door for her to seek the attention that she needed. When I learned of the affair we tried to reconcile our marriage. Anne was clearly fed up. She left California without me and moved back to Maryland. I was devastated.

After my wife left me, my world collapsed into a dark place. I didn't want to do comedy. I didn't want to hang out. I just wanted my wife back in my life. I found myself crying a lot and staying home. Now that I was alone, things became difficult to manage. I tried to stick with it and fly solo but I soon became overwhelmed. My ambition to succeed was replaced by suicidal thoughts and constant tears. Nothing in my life had prepared me to deal with having my wife walk out on me. I tried to recover from the heartbreak but nothing else mattered to me. I couldn't put the pieces back together and being in California became a burden. I made the decision to drop everything and retreat to a safe place. I called my mother and let her know that I would be coming back home. I packed up my things and left California behind me. I needed to be embraced by the love of my family to help me heal again.

Chapter 15

Home Again

The 1980s was a decade that can be defined by hundreds of events that changed the course of history in our country. Reganomics, The Cold War, the domination of pop music, the video game craze, the rise of the Hip-Hop culture and the Stock Market crash are just a few events that made a permanent impact on our society. Within the poverty-stricken neighborhoods of the inner-city there was another phenomenon that unleashed destruction like a tidal wave. The epidemic of Crack and Powder Cocaine attacked those communities like nothing we had ever seen before. Suddenly thousands of people found themselves caught in the fatal cycle of drug addiction and criminal prosecutions. The Crack Epidemic claimed thousands of lives and destroyed families and communities from all over the nation.

I first learned of the dangers of crack and cocaine early in my life. Back in Maryland I went to school with a young basketball phenom by the name of Len Bias. He was an amazing talent who later graduated and played for the University of Maryland. Len Bias was not only a local hero, but his outstanding play and unmatched skills caught the eye of Boston Celtic President Red Auerbach. The legendary coach and executive had been watching Len Bias for his entire college career. Len Bias entered the draft after his senior year and the Boston Celtics selected him as the 2nd overall pick. We were beyond excited to see a local legend elevate to the heights of becoming a NBA player for a storied franchise. But Len Bias would never play a minute of basketball for the Boston Celtics.

Less than forty-eight hours after being drafted, Len Bias decided to come back to his dorm at the University of Maryland to celebrate his arrival to the NBA. He partied with a few of his teammates and members of the university's football team. Later that evening Len Bias went to a smaller gathering off campus with a group of his friends. He was offered drugs and Len Bias decided to try it. After taking the cocaine Len Bias began to have seizures and he passed out. Tragically Len Bias never regained consciousness. The twenty-two year old legend died just a few hours later.

The story of Len Bias and his terrible death is just one of the countless tragedies that highlighted the ripple effects of the crack epidemic. During the mid to late 80's, the nightly news coverage featured dozens of stories about gang violence, drug related deaths and family destruction because of the crisis. I always feared the dangers of drugs and the Len Bias story was another harsh reminder. I never wanted to be exposed to the perilous lifestyle that came with being addicted. Throughout my life I have been able to avoid the temptations of drug abuse. Unfortunately, my brother Henry was not so lucky.

After separating from my wife and coming back to Maryland, I was faced with an uphill battle. The depressing feeling of suddenly becoming single again weighed heavy on me. My family had never seen me so despondent. Every morning brought a new challenge to pick myself up from the lowest point in my life and regain my confidence. Once I settled back into life on the east coast I headed to see the one person I knew could cheer me up whenever I was down on myself—my older brother Henry.

Seeing my brother again made me realize that I wasn't the only one that was dealing with tough times. I found my brother near the National Mall in the tourist section of Washington, D.C. Henry was selling designer shades to the out-of-towners. He was making good money but I was shocked to see him as a street vendor. His appearance had changed and I could tell something deeper was happening to my brother. Henry's life had begun to spin out of control from a decision he'd made just a few years back.

While running his own contracting business Henry was approached by a friend who worked for his company. He asked Henry to borrow some money so he could make an investment. Henry agreed to lend his friend the money. When his friend repaid the loan and doubled Henry's money, my brother became intrigued. He found out that his friend was selling crack cocaine. From that day forward Henry entered the destructive world of drug addiction. His life would never been the same. My brother became a crack addict that same year. His business suffered and he eventually lost everything. His family was devastated by his decision. Henry found himself getting evicted and living in shelters with his family. The sickness of being a drug addict became so strong that Henry lost it all. He lost his wife and kids, and eventually found himself living on the streets. When I returned home I couldn't believe how much had changed while I was living in California. While I was chasing my dreams and mingling with the celebrities in Hollywood, I was unaware that my brother was suffering in the streets back home.

It didn't take long for Henry's crack addiction to take over his life. Henry found himself being arrested for petty crimes that quickly escalated into a string of serious felonies. Henry spent six years of his life incarcerated. He spent stretches in Lorton Reformatory and Hagerstown Correctional Facility. I hated seeing my brother locked up. I knew Henry had a multitude of talents and witnessing his life waste away was heartbreaking for me. Although Henry and I are blood brothers, we are total opposites in multiple areas in our lives. While I was always a tall and lanky kid, Henry was athletic with natural abilities. He was always better than me in sports. Henry is also an amazing artist. He can sit down and sketch anything he lays his eyes on, with amazing precision. When it came time to fix something around the house, everyone in the family would call on Henry. He was always good with his hands.

When crack cocaine took over his decisions, Henry became a different person. He started to care less about having a normal life. He no longer wanted the responsibility of raising a family and holding down a regular job. If my brother was not in the prison system, he was living as a vagrant throughout the city. Being homeless became a daily way of life for my brother. During those hot summer days my brother was living on the streets. During those cold winter nights my brother was living on the streets. He slept in back alleys, tunnels and even behind the government buildings. It was hard for me to believe it. The man that I looked up to my entire life was one of the thousands of homeless people that roamed our nation's capital.

My brother's reality became an eye opening experience for me. Henry had a serious crack addiction. His need to get high was something that he battled with every day. We always argued about his lifestyle. Trying to convince him to get off the streets became a part of our daily discussions. We would have shouting matches and heated arguments constantly. Henry would tell me that he didn't see the need for him to stop being homeless. Henry pointed to the fact that I was struggling in my own life. My brother said that I was working hard to pay bills and that was something that he didn't have to worry about. He told me that being a homeless person was his decision. Henry wasn't the only person who believed that. My brother met dozens of friends that lived on the streets and each one of them made the decision to engage that lifestyle.

I spoke with a lot of Henry's friends and they were all good guys. They were not the typical homeless people that you see in the movies. They were all smart and intelligent individuals who decided to live on the streets and remove themselves from the responsibilities of everyday life. Most of Henry's homeless friends had families and places to go. They were not forced to live on the streets. They simply chose to be homeless. Henry and his friends even had girlfriends that were living with them on the streets. It was an entire world that boggled my mind. Many of them left well-paying jobs and found themselves being homeless once the drug addiction took over. They had to beg, borrow and steal whenever they could in order to support their habit. My brother, however, went another route.

Henry was born with a natural gift of gab. He was never afraid to talk to anyone. Henry's personality could attract people from all walks of life. When it was time for Henry to earn money he became a street vendor. My brother sold handbags, shades, umbrellas, watches, gold chains and anything else he could get his hands on. When he needed his fix, Henry would head down to the National Mall and sell just about anything to the tourists. The money didn't last long. Sometimes he would make thousands of dollars in just a few days just to blow it all on drugs. His nonstop decline affected our entire family.

When I returned from California it seemed that my brother and I spent every day together. While I was trying to mend the shattered pieces of my life, my brother was right there to encourage me when he could. We leaned on each other for support. When I was frustrated about my life and it seemed that I was unable to cope, Henry was right there to give me advice. When I would find Henry on the street I would drive by, and pick him up.. Although we were battling different demons we truly needed each other during that time.

Our relationship has always been that way. Henry and I lifted each other throughout our lives. Even as we became men, Henry never stopped being my big brother. He always looked out for me. I remember one day we were walking and my brother noticed that my shoe was untied. He told me to stop walking for a second and knelt down in front of me. My brother tied my shoe and made sure that I wouldn't trip and fall. Even as a grown man, Henry still looked out for me. His small gesture was a huge reminder that Henry would always be there when I needed him. I could never ask for a more genuine big brother.

Henry's crack addiction went on for years. My family tried everything to get help for my brother. There were days when I blamed my father for Henry's problems. I believed that if my dad had been there for us, Henry would not have been exposed to this downward spiral. I was angry with my father for years. But the truth was clear for Henry. He needed to make the decision to change his life on his own. We continued to plead with him to leave the drugs alone. Like millions of families across the nation we found ourselves reeling from the disparaging effects of drugs. My brother Henry wasn't himself during those years. It was sad to see him destroy everything he had built. No amount of love or scrutiny made Henry change his mind. His addiction was too strong. My brother spent nearly two decades of his life as a homeless addict. It took an unspeakable tragedy to finally wake him up and convince Henry to leave the dangerous life behind him.

Chapter 16

Sulei

After being back in Maryland for nearly two years I continued to find myself picking up the pieces after my failed marriage. Anne and I never reconciled our union and we eventually divorced. Despite my rocky personal life, my professional career was in a good place. I eventually regained my focus and returned to the stage. I worked the east coast club circuit and booked several headlining gigs. I wasn't fully over my wife, but I knew deep down inside that I needed to move on.

One night I was in my local supermarket when I notice an attractive woman near the produce section. I had seen thousands of beautiful ladies in my life but there was something that instantly attracted me to her. Since my teenage years I had never gotten over my hesitation to approach the opposite sex. Lucky for me, this exotic woman was far from shy. She noticed that I was gazing at her and she spoke to me. We talked for a few minutes and I walked her to her car. I couldn't get over how amazing she was. Physically, she was the total package— attractive, tall and fit. She was from Brazil and her accent was as thick as her curves. Her name was Sulei Santos.

The chances of Sulei and I meeting were well beyond a million to one shot. Sulei was raised in one of the poorest sections of Rio de Janeiro. Hearing her story only deepened my attraction to her. Sulei told me about her life and how she made it to the United States. Back in Brazil, her family had been extremely poor. She explained how her family lived near a beach, in one of the poorest ghettos of the city. She described her house as having cardboard and tin siding with dirt floors. The conditions were horrible. Sulei worked for a dance troupe back home. She was the breadwinner for the family. She did everything to help take care of her mom, grandmother and her siblings. Sulei worked under some of the worse conditions imaginable. She was sexually abused and constantly harassed by her own boss. When Sulei got chosen to come to America for a performance, she decided to seize the opportunity to escape to a better life.

Sulei and her dance troupe were scheduled to perform at the Warner Theater in Washington, D.C. In the middle of the performance Sulei decided that her moment had arrived. Sulei and her best friend escaped out the back door of the Warner Theater. They bolted into the busy streets and never looked back. Sulei made up her mind that she would never return to the country known today as the murder capital of the world. Sulei roamed the streets of Washington, D.C. without a clue of which direction to turn. Sulei barely knew the language and knew nothing about the city. God was surely with her that evening because Sulei met a sympathetic woman in the Georgetown section. The woman decided to take her in.

By the time I met Sulei, she had been in the United States for some years. She had learned English and worked like a dog to make a better life for herself. She started working as a waitress at a gentleman's club. Before long, Sulei became an exotic dancer making thousands of dollars per week. I didn't mind her choice of occupation because I had dated strippers and models before. I admired the person she was and the risk she had taken to start her life over again.

On our first date Sulei invited me over to her place for a home cooked meal. I was taken aback by the gesture. Of all the women I dated in the past no one had ever cooked dinner for me on the first date. But Sulei was a very different person. From the day we met, Sulei treated me like a king. She was a very generous woman. Our relationship moved very fast. It only took a few months of dating before I found myself moving in with her. After my heartbreaking experience in California I needed someone in my life that genuinely loved me, and that person was Sulei.

When I was booked for my road gigs, my new girlfriend traveled with me. All of my comedian friends got a kick out of her. Sulei could light up a room when she walked in. Her voluptuous stature commanded attention in any setting. I had to be a very secure man when we were out in public. Men would walk up to her and offer her business cards everywhere we went. It didn't matter if I was standing right next to her. Thirsty men would press their luck and try to come between what we had. Sulei was proud of her body and she wasn't afraid to flaunt her good looks. I didn't mind the attention she got from most men. But some attention she received was downright dangerous.

When I came into Sulei's life she was a few years removed from a destructive marriage. She told me that she was afraid of her ex-husband who had been verbally abusive to her in recent years. Because they had a son together, Sulei found herself in an impossible situation. Her ex-husband would berate and threaten her constantly. He wanted her back so he tried to bully her into reconciling their marriage. But Sulei had grown tired of his abusive ways. She eventually started dating a police officer from Washington, D.C. A lot of off-duty cops frequented the club she danced in. That is where she met her new friend. Because he was a policeman, Sulei finally felt protected. What Sulei didn't know was that the officer she met was a dirty cop from the area. He made the local news for being named in a citywide corruption sting. As Sulei and I became close, she began to ease him out of the picture, but the officer refused to let her go. He would come to the club and watch her. Sometimes he would park his car outside of her apartment and stalk her. Sulei waited until we dated a few times to give me the news. I was unaware that the corrupt cop was watching us on multiple occasions. Because of my martial arts background, I had always considered myself a badass. I knew that I could handle myself in most situations. But fighting with a dirty cop was one encounter that I knew I wouldn't live through to tell the story. I became more cautious about my surroundings. Looking over my shoulders became second nature. I paid attention to every car that passed in front of me and stayed vigilant when I was in traffic. When I visited Sulei at the strip club, the dirty cop would be sitting at the bar. He clearly knew that Sulei and I were an item.

A few months later Sulei became my second wife. We didn't have a huge wedding but we wanted to make our marriage special. Sulei told everyone at the club. The news quickly spread that she was officially Mrs. Sulei Lee. The dirty cop got wind of our wedding and finally backed down. He realized that Sulei was now in a serious relationship and he eventually disappeared from the picture. We never saw him again.

Sulei was a hard worker. That was one of the things I admired about her. She didn't play when it came to her money. She was serious about saving and building a better life for her and her family. People laugh when they hear strippers talk about putting themselves through school by dancing. But that was Sulei. She earned a lot of money and wisely invested in herself. Sulei ensured that she never had to live like she did back in Brazil. When it was time to move from her apartment, Sulei relocated into a nice townhome that she bought with cash.

For the first two years of our marriage Sulei and I had an amazing time. I became close with her young son. I played basketball with him and gave him life advice whenever I could. Sulei and I slowly started to build our life together. Having her with me on the road was always fun. My wife was in love with my stage act and she would do anything to support me. Sulei soon became obsessed with helping to guide my career. She was doing very well as a dancer and she made boat loads of cash. She used her resources and invested in me. Sulei bought me outfits to wear on stage. She even hired a hair stylist to give me a mini-makeover before some of my shows. I knew my wife meant well and she just wanted me to succeed. But her constant pressure started to make me feel uneasy.

After Sulei left the strip club in Washington, D.C., things began to change with our relationship. She found a new job at a gentleman's club near Baltimore with a more affluent clientele. She was now dancing for wealthy men and they loved her. Sometimes we joked about how old and rich men would tip her thousands of dollars just to sit and listen to their problems. They would rant about their wives and how they were unhappy at home. Sulei couldn't believe the amount of money she was making. One day a baseball player from the Baltimore Orioles came into the club. When he met Sulei he was immediately smitten. Unbeknownst to me, my wife started a friendship with the player. She managed to keep it a secret for some time. When I found out about him, things quickly spiraled out of control.

Sulei tried her best to convince me that nothing was happening between them. My wife told me that the player invited her to a party on his yacht and also offered to buy her a luxury car. Sulei constantly communicated with the player. They would call each other behind my back and their friendship only infuriated me. My wife would never give me the player's name. She feared that I would track him down or go to the press with the story of how the MLB player was destroying my marriage. Sulei and I had countless arguments about her new friend. The heated exchanges would be filled with accusations and even violent threats. Her unwillingness to end the friendship would push me over the edge. I never laid hands on my wife but the arguments would send me into a violent rage. I would punch a hole in the wall or turn over a bed when the arguments became too much. On one occasion I even put my hand through a glass window out of anger and nearly broke my arm. The physical scars from the stitches are still visible today. As my wife's inappropriate friendship continued, our arguments only escalated. One evening Sulei became fearful to the point of calling the police on me. I left the house before the authorities arrived but I eventually turned myself in. I was charged with domestic violence because of the threats I made out of anger. The charges were eventually dropped and my wife and I tried to make things better. But the damage was already done.

I moved out of Sulei's townhouse and rented a small condo in Silver Springs, Maryland. I needed desperately to regain my freedom. The love I had for my second wife was dwindling as old feelings of resentment and betrayal started consuming me. I didn't realize it at the time but I was not fully over the heartbreak of my first marriage.

The suppressed anger I felt from a childhood littered with abuse also began to play a role in my frustrations. I was emotionally drained from all of the energy I spent trying to make my marriage work. I felt myself losing focus on my career again and realized that I needed to make a change.

One evening I was working at a jazz club in Maryland. I was separated from my wife so I started seeing other women. I was convinced that Sulei was having an affair so I didn't see a problem with cheating on her. I ended up meeting a waitress at the club and we became close. I needed someone to take my mind off of Sulei so I allowed the woman to move into my condo. The waitress and I spent a lot of time together. In fact, she tagged along with me one Sunday when I visited a church with my family. My mother met my new girlfriend and told my wife that I was seeing another woman. It didn't take long for Sulei to contact me. She told me how much she missed me and how she wanted to make our marriage work again. I loved my wife so I agreed to give us another chance.

A few weeks later I was back living with Sulei. Things were good for a few months. We tried hard to have fun together and rekindle the intense attraction we once had. But things were too far gone. Our destructive pattern resumed once I discovered that my wife and the baseball player were back in contact with each other. The violent arguments continued and we found ourselves at odds with each other. After an ugly shouting match, I stormed out of her home. We both had clearly had enough. I drove through the night and eventually pulled over in a dark parking lot. I needed to cool down. I was left to deal with the tough reality that another marriage was over. I knew that Sulei and I loved each other but the trust between us was gone. It was sad to watch our passion grow cold, but ultimately it was for the best. I can honestly say that we are both better people for crossing paths with each other.

Chapter 17

Solina

There's a good reason why people still use the old saying that blood is thicker than water. In most cases, no one is going to support you and be there for you like your own flesh and blood. Ever since we were kids, my mother always taught us to value our family. Her lessons have guided me well into my adult years. There were times in my life when I questioned the true motives of a few family members. I was unsure if certain relatives truly loved and cared for me. But as I matured over the years, my mother's advice regarding family became crystal clear. When I returned home from California only to witness how my brother had lost his family, I empathized with his pain. Now that I was single again, thoughts of my own child started to consume me. I was ready to move on with my life, but I was still missing a major part of me. I thought about Solina a lot. I wondered where she was and if she was healthy and safe. After nearly six years and two failed marriages I was ready to find my daughter.

Every time I thought about how to find Solina I would hit a major road block. I had lost contact with Solina's legal guardian when she was just in diapers. The last phone number I had for Solina's mother was disconnected. I grew frustrated and didn't know where to turn. I was all out of options until my cousin approached me with an idea. He explained to me how the internet was becoming a great tool to stay in touch with people. He told me that I could do a search for Solina's mother and there was a good chance I would find her. I was clueless when it came to the internet. I had rarely used search engines back then, but I was willing to give it a try. I searched for my daughter's mother, and shockingly her full name popped up on the screen. There was a phone number listed for Venus in Galax, Virginia. I immediately picked up the phone and dialed the number. The phone rang a few times before a familiar voice answered the line.

"Venus?" I asked.

"Hello," My daughter's mother responded. "Is this Kevin?"

"Yes," I sharply said. "Where the hell have you been? I've been looking all over for you."

"I'm in Virginia." Venus replied. "I have your daughter here. Do you want to speak with her?"

Venus handed Solina the phone. When I heard her voice, I was instantly relieved. I couldn't believe that after all these years, a simple Google search reconnected me with my daughter. When Venus returned to the phone I told her that I wanted to see Solina as soon as possible. She agreed and gave me the address to her apartment. I had never heard of Galax, Virginia but I was willing to travel through Hell and high water to see Solina again.

A lot of things had changed with Venus since we last spoke. She had met a man while she was in job core and decided to move to Galax with him. She had two more kids by other men and she was struggling to maintain her family. The State of Virginia had allowed her to take full custody of Solina and her other children. However, Venus was under a watchful eye because of her sketchy history of child abandonment. I was eager to spend time with my daughter so I took the twelve-hour bus ride to see her. When I arrived to the small town just north of Tennessee I couldn't believe my eyes.

Galax, Virginia reminded me of Mayberry from the Andy Griffith Show. The town wasn't big at all. Galax is a total of eight square miles with a total population of less than seven thousand residents. The people there were quite different from what I was used to back in Maryland. In fact, when I reunited with my daughter I couldn't believe how country she was. I hadn't seen her in years so it was strange to see her speaking like a Nashville native. I spent the entire weekend in Galax. Venus' family was the only black family in the town so it was interesting to hang out with my daughter in that area.

I took her to the movies and out for ice cream so that I could get to know her again. She was a lot different than I expected. She was a black girl and she looked like me, but the small country town had made a huge impression on her personality.

I drove back and forth to Galax a number of times to see my daughter that year. I was always happy to spend time with her. Being around Solina again was the breath of fresh air that I needed. I remember Solina telling me that she would ask her mom about her daddy. Venus would tell her daughter that I was probably dead. It was good to reassure her that her dad was back in her life to stay. Solina was smart and full of life. To say that I was proud to be her father is an understatement. I took her shopping and made sure that she had everything she needed before I took the drive back to Maryland.

Venus wasn't doing well financially back then. As I spent more time in Galax, I realized that she was struggling mightily to raise her kids. She had a new boyfriend in the small town but they were not earning enough to support their large household. I tried to help out as much as I could but it wasn't long before I learned that Venus' issues were deeper than just money.

One day Solina loaded her younger brother into a small wagon and left Venus' apartment. My daughter walked from house to house and started knocking on the doors. She was hungry and she needed food. She tried to find anyone in the neighborhood that would help her. Before long, Solina found herself on the doorstep of a sympathetic family. She explained to them that her mother had left all of the kids alone and went to another state. Solina hadn't eaten and she was starving. The family was shocked by the story. They fed my daughter and her little brother. They also called the police. Child Protective Services arrived the same day and took all of the kids, including Solina. When Venus returned to Galax she was immediately arrested.

A few days later I received a hysterical call from my daughter's mother. She told me that the State of Virginia had taken all of her kids and she was losing full custody. I instantly became furious. I couldn't believe my ears. Venus was crying uncontrollably. She told me that

I needed to contact the court if I wanted to gain custody of Solina before it was too late. I didn't want my daughter to get trapped into the foster care system. She needed to be around her family, so I did everything in my power to make that happen.

I contacted the court and began the process of gaining custody of Solina. I submitted everything from tax documents, letters from my agents and managers and I even submitted blood samples to confirm that I was the biological father. The process was tedious and it took some time but I was willing to do anything for my daughter. Because Venus had four children from four different men, the judge requested the appearance of each one of us.

I was there at every court appearance for Solina. I did everything that was asked of me to ensure that we would get a favorable ruling. A few weeks later I received the news that I had been waiting for. I was so excited to receive the news that I was granted full custody of Solina. I was always uneasy about Solina being in Galax. There were so many struggling families in the area. There was a visible drug crisis in Galax and most of the kids were exposed to a questionable future. After all the years of not knowing where my daughter was I was finally able to bring her back to Maryland and give her the upbringing she deserved.

Solina had to adjust to her new life in the DMV. She had been around country white people her entire life and I could tell that she was uncomfortable around her own people. When I introduced Solina to her aunts, uncle and cousins I noticed that she was uneasy. She had never been around so many black people before. Her heavy accent was just the tip of the iceberg. Solina knew nothing about black culture. I was even shocked to learn that she was unaware of who Michael Jackson was. I spoke to Solina every day about her identity. I wanted to raise my daughter like my mother raised me. When I was young I was taught to love everyone, no matter the color of their skin. But it was mandatory that I learned about myself and my culture. I taught Solina about Martin Luther King, Jr. and Malcolm X. I gave her lessons about Africa and what it meant to be a black person in

America. I let my daughter know that she could date anyone from any cultural background, as long as they treated her good. I didn't want her to go through life and not understand her culture and where she came from. It took a number of years but my daughter became more comfortable around her family and her people.

Having Solina back home and around her family was a major life change for me. I was raising Solina along with her older sister Genee. When the court asked all the fathers to be present at each of our hearings, unfortunately Genee's father never showed up. The court suggested putting her in a foster home. I agreed to take custody of Genee and help raise her. Solina and Genee were close so I figured it would be better to keep them together. I enrolled the sisters into the P.G. County school district and we started our lives together. It was a challenging change of pace for me, so I did everything I could for the girls.

No matter how much love I gave to Solina she continued to miss her mother immensely. I always treated my daughter like a princess and gave her everything she needed. But the one thing I could never give her was her mother's love. Solina would mention Venus all the time and ask me if she could go back to Galax. I couldn't understand why she wanted to return to Virginia but I knew she was missing a piece of her that only her mother could fill.

After Venus' life began to stabilize, the court granted her visitation rights to come see the girls in Maryland. She visited me a few times and stayed at my apartment with the kids. I could tell that Venus was still having problems. It was hard for her to completely pull things back together. The men in her life were still causing issues and Venus developed an obvious drug habit. But despite her problems, Solina and Genee were always happy to see their mother.

One day Venus decided to come to Maryland to visit us. She wasn't traveling alone on this particular trip and I found that odd. She told me that she wanted to see her children and I agreed. When I greeted Venus I noticed she was with a white guy who reminded me of a hardcore punk rocker. They were planning to stay for a few days and I didn't have a problem with that. When Solina and Genee went to school that next morning I headed out to run some errands and take care of some business. I didn't realize it at the time but Venus had a more devious reason for her Maryland visit.

While my daughter and Genee were in school, Venus and her boyfriend checked them out of classes early. They stole the sisters and drove them back to Virginia. By the time I learned that my child was missing, Venus was long gone. I was beyond livid. I had full custody of my daughter so now Venus had graduated to being a kidnapper. I immediately called down to Galax but her number was out of service. For the third time in my life I had lost total contact with my daughter.

Nearly three excruciating months went by with no word from Venus. I continued to reach out and kept coming up empty. No one had seen or heard from Venus or her boyfriend. One night, just after midnight, my mother received a frantic call. It was Genee. She was crying on the other line. Genee and my mother had gotten close since she arrived in Maryland and she memorized my mother's phone number.

"Genee, where are you?" My mother quickly asked.

"We are in Georgia." Genee cried on the other line. "I am with my mom and her boyfriend and they have no money for a hotel. My mom's boyfriend is trying to make me sell my body."

"What!?" My mother yelled into the phone. "Where is Solina?"

"She is in Galax." Genee responded. "One of her teachers took her in and now she stays with their family."

My mother couldn't believe the news. She immediately called me and we contacted Solina's teacher in Galax. Solina had been living with the family for months now. She didn't know my number so she had no way of contacting us. The next morning I got on the road and took the seven hour ride to Galax. I rescued my daughter yet again and this time I was never going to let her go. Venus and her boyfriend were later arrested for a number of unrelated charges and she did some jail time. Solina was beyond ecstatic to be with me again. One day she told me that she now realized that she is better off staying with me than with her crazy mom.

Genee sadly moved from one foster home to another for most of her teenage years. She developed major behavior issues. Family after family returned her to the system. They couldn't handle her. Genee was later arrested and sentenced to a women's correctional facility in Virginia. Solina and I visited her, and seeing her condition made my heart ache. I realized that Solina could have easily ended up in the same position if things were different. I will always be grateful for how life turned out for my daughter.

Genee eventually got her life back on track. She went back to school and now her life is in an amazing place. She's married and she has started a family. I'm very proud of her. Solina and her mother lost contact for many years. Once Venus was released from jail, she too put the pieces of her life back together slowly. She contacted my daughter through social media and they started to mend their relationship. Venus attended Solina's college graduation and it was good to see their relationship in a better place.

Fighting for Solina is something I would never trade for anything in this world. When I was just a toddler my mother fought to make her family whole again. Throughout her life I have watched my mom work tirelessly to ensure that her kids were taken care of. I always wanted to do the same for Solina. Raising a daughter as a single man was never an easy task. Our journey together was far from perfect. Solina and I have seen some of the happiest days our lives together. And unfortunately, we have also shared some tragedies. Having my daughter back in my life was all that mattered to me. Making the decision to find her is something I would never regret.

Chapter 18

My Calling

It is hard for me to imagine life without my daughter Solina. When she returned to Maryland, Solina filled a void I never knew existed. Once I gained full custody of my child I realized that things were going to change. Becoming a full-time father meant that I had to reevaluate my life and make the necessary changes to ensure that Solina was well taken care of. When I took inventory of my situation I was confronted with a humbling dilemma. *How do I juggle my career around the reality of being a single dad?* Ironically, I found the answer within my question. To successfully raise my daughter and chase my dreams I would have to lean on my talent of juggling.

Although I was mentally prepared to take care of Solina, I was far from financially stable. My career was in the doldrums. I was booking shows sporadically, but the club gigs were not paying enough money to make a decent living. The greedy agents and club owners of that time started to take a toll on the industry. A lot of comedians felt the pinch of less gigs and lower pay. I grew tired of feeding my daughter Ramen Noodles every night. We seemed to eat Hot Pockets and Ramen Noodles all the time. Through it all, my daughter never complained. She knew her dad was working hard to give her a better life. As the club dates became few and far between, I knew that I had to come up with a plan.

I thought back to the time when I lived in California in the early 90s. In order to make ends meet while I waited on a big Hollywood gig, I became a street performer. I set up shop on the world-famous Venice Beach and performed daily for tourists coming from all over the world. When I joined the sub culture of street performing, I was amazed how many people worked on the beaches for a living. Most of the street performers and vendors never worked a full-time job. They were serious about their craft. I learned a lot of tricks to the trade while I was in California. I also made a lot of money. Now that I was back on the east coast I decided it was time to become a street performer again. Because I was very familiar with the DC area, I knew that millions of people traveled to the nation's capital every year. I chose the National Mall as my spot.

For nearly seven years I performed on the National Mall as a juggler and comedian. I would take a small bag of props downtown and set up shop. I entertained tourists as they walked by and took pictures of the historical structures in the area. I placed a bucket a few feet from me and gave the crowd a quick five-minute show. Some people would stop and watch my set. Some people would tip me and throw money into my bucket. Some people would take photos of me. Other people would walk by and ignore me like I was invisible. Some people would even say mean and nasty things to me for no apparent reason. People would mistake me for a homeless person because I was juggling on the National Mall.

One day a young kid took a video of me while I was doing my juggling set. He posted the video online a few days later. I found the video and was shocked by the message. The caption described his experience of seeing a homeless bum juggling while he was visiting Washington, DC. The post insulted me. The young kid along with scores of clueless people had a terrible misconception about me and other street performers across the nation. There are thousands of street performers who are homeless and have no other means to earn a living. However, I was not one of those people. Street vending and performing is a very big business throughout the world. I was in a prime location near the National Mall and it was a lucrative business for me. I could no longer rely on the income from the comedy clubs. There were times during the peak season when I would make thousands of dollars in just one weekend. I didn't mind braving the elements because the money was good. Dozens of people would stop to watch me and tip me for my juggling. I enjoyed meeting the people and taking pictures with them. The fans that understood my drive made it easier for me to deal with the assholes who would mumble insults and look down on me. Those people had no clue that I was far from homeless. They didn't know that I was juggling to take care of my daughter and push my career.

When Solina was not in school I would take her down to the National Mall with me. She would sit off to the side or near a park bench where I could see her. She would watch the tourist walk by and throw money into her daddy's bucket. The money helped us a lot. When my daughter and I returned home from those long days we would empty the bucket onto the living room floor and count the money. My daughter would help me place the coins into a bank wrapper and line up the dollars. Counting up to two, three and even four hundred dollars each day was normal for us back in those days. Because of the street performing, I never felt compelled to get a full-time job. Being on the National Mall gave me an opportunity to take care of my daughter and still have time to book more club dates. Although the money was coming in fast during my days of street performing, it always seemed as if it was never enough. I was always behind on our bills. Having our electricity, cable or phone shut off became a monthly carousel of frustration for us. Because of the lack of a steady paycheck I couldn't afford to give my daughter everything her heart desired. For a long time, to simply survive without losing our apartment became a good month for us.

During the off-peak season for tourism in Washington, DC I found myself doing longer hours down at the National Mall. I had to keep my head above water and keep the money coming in. Going from performing on national television and touring overseas, to now performing for dollars on the street was no easy transition for me. I was quietly making more money than I was earning throughout the comedy club circuit but the perception that I was a homeless man was a hard pill to swallow. I have always been a performer with a large ego. Despite my nationwide exposure, people looked at me differently when I was on the street, especially the police officers.

I have been arrested a half-dozen times by The United States Park Police for juggling on the National Mall. One officer even arrested me twice in one week. I would spend a few hours in custody and the authorities would eventually let me out. One day I was forced to spend the night in jail for juggling. I remember a few inmates recognized me from television while I was inside. The ridiculous charges were always dropped, and I was required to pay a fine. No matter how many times I was arrested I always returned to the same location and continued my performances. I needed to support my family and I never let a few hours in jail deter me.

As I started to get back into the comedy clubs I had to make more adjustments in my life. When no one was available to watch Solina for me, I would take her to some of the performances with me. Some nights I would have my daughter stay in the hotel rooms alone. If I didn't want her to stay by herself I would bring her to the comedy clubs with me. Solina would wait in the kitchen or in a back room until I was done with my set. I didn't want my daughter to hear the vulgar language of the other comedians. Despite having to take Solina with me I still wanted to protect her at all costs.

Being a single dad forced me to become creative about balancing my home and my career. I didn't have all the answers when it came time for me to care for my daughter. As a male trying to raise a young girl there were no shortage of challenges. My sisters Dawn and Brigette always stepped in when I needed their help with my daughter. I remember Solina coming home from school one day and informing me that she had just gotten her period for the first time. What was supposed to be a simple trip to the pharmacy turned into a big debate between Brigette and I about the best feminine products to buy for Solina. I needed to have those conversations with my sisters at that time. They gave me information that I would have never learned on my own. I not only had to teach and raise my daughter, but I also had to learn as much as I could to be the best father I could be for her.

I taught my daughter everything I knew about life to help her become a good person. Like every man raising a daughter I taught her about the types of boys to avoid and the importance of her education. Because I was abused and assaulted when I was very young, I wanted to teach my daughter how to protect herself. I taught her many martial arts lessons and the basics of self-defense. I got my old Karate equipment out of the closet and taught her how to punch, kick and block. When Solina was younger I spent a few nights per week teaching her the techniques that I learned and taught before she was born. She would enjoy her lessons and it was a great time for us to bond. I knew that I couldn't be there to protect her forever. As she became a mature young woman I just wanted her to be able to handle herself.

My family absolutely adored Solina. They loved to babysit her and have my daughter over their houses. Some relatives even offered to take custody of Solina. They were aware of my hectic professional career and felt that they could give my daughter a better upbringing. Many relatives questioned the fact that I was a single man and if I would have the time and the resources to raise Solina. When my new girlfriends would visit and meet my daughter they were eager to try and fill the role of Solina's guardian. On a few occasions I allowed my girlfriends to stay with Solina while I traveled on tour dates. However, none of the women could replace Solina's need for her real mother. My sisters stepped in to watch Solina when I was away, but they also couldn't replace Solina's mother. Because Solina's mother was in and out of her life, I did everything I could to give Solina the unlimited love and support that she deserved.

When Solina was younger it took us many years to understand each other. We've had our share of struggles and disagreements over the years. I've always felt the pressure of having to earn enough money to support her. In addition to the financial support, I always wanted to give her the emotional and practical nurturing to help her make the right decisions in life. When Solina entered her mid-teens, and became more interested in boys, our relationship changed. One day while she was in school I walked by her room and noticed that her computer was on. On a normal day I would've ignored her screen but that particular day I noticed the word "clinic" from the corner of my eye. My curiosity got the best of me and I started going through her computer. What I discovered shocked me. My daughter Solina was sexually active and had been for some time. I could never believe in a million years that my daughter would lose her virginity on my watch. I was living in a fantasy world for a long time when it came to Solina. I believed that she was going to be virgin until she found the right man and got married. Reading the proof of my daughter's sex life became a harsh dose of reality for me. I broke down and cried in front of the computer. I realized the days of tucking in my little girl were over and she was becoming a woman. I didn't talk to my daughter for two weeks after finding the news on her computer. I was disappointed in Solina. I couldn't bring myself to believe the news. My daughter had always been a good kid. It took a while for me to understand her decision. I had to accept the fact that she was growing up. Although I disagreed with her timing, I encouraged my daughter to be careful. I just wanted her to think about her future and make better choices with her life.

As Solina became a young woman and eventually graduated high school, our relationship had evolved into an amazing place. Through our love, our battles and our lessons Solina unknowingly made me a better father and a better person. There is no question that we drove each other crazy when she was younger. Having been thrust into a different world of living with her dad was surely a change that was hard for Solina to deal with. After years of really getting to know each other I'm proud of where our journey together has taken us.

Chapter 19

Dawn

Throughout my life it seems that drugs have been an inescapable part of my journey. I've spent most of my life turning down countless offers to exchange a few hours of euphoria for years of drug addiction. For as long as I could remember I have always been cautious about smoking, sniffing and even drinking. I credit a lot of my healthy ways to studying Martial Arts when I was just a young boy. I've also seen how the Crack Era has affected so many people. It's an old cliché but the meaning remains true. Drugs don't discriminate. Addiction can hit any family regardless of income status. Drugs don't respect borders. It doesn't avoid people based on their race or gender. The problem of drug addiction is never isolated to just the abuser. It has a ripple effect throughout the family. The outcome of being mixed up in this dangerous lifestyle can have disastrous consequences. Every day I wish that I could say that my family has not been shattered by the drug epidemic. While my brother Henry was suffering with his addiction, my younger sister was also caught in the grips of this treacherous world.

Ever since we were kids, my sister Dawn has always been a good person and full of life. Anyone who knew Dawn, when she was just a little girl, knew that she had a good spirit and could light up any room. The young girl who was infatuated with Michael Jackson has always been the type of person who just wanted to have fun. Because Dawn was a few years younger than me, we didn't hang out much. Outside of being my magician's assistance when we were kids, Dawn and I had our own lives. By the time my sister reached high school she was hanging with her own friends and learning some tough lessons about life.

As Dawn moved into her twenties, she began to hang around the wrong crowd. She dated a few street guys and became introduced to the dangerous drug world. My sister eventually developed a bad drug habit and found herself wrapped up with the wrong element. Dawn battled with her addiction for years. Even when she started her own family, Dawn couldn't escape the web of friends that kept her entrenched in this perilous world. Drug dealers constantly came in and out of my sister's life. Dawn became romantically involved with some of the dealers and other dealers were just so-called friends. On August 6, 2010, my baby sister found herself caught up in a situation that changed our family forever. It was a day I will never forget for the rest of my life.

My day started off just like many other Friday during that summer in the DMV. I was headed down to the National Mall to set up my area for a long day of street performing. It was a gorgeous morning. The bright sun lit up the city and it wasn't a dark cloud in the sky. I drove around the area a few times and searched for my brother Henry. He worked downtown and I always checked on him when I knew he was in the area. Before I found my brother, I got a frantic call from my sister Brigette.

I had never heard my big sister so distraught. She was crying uncontrollably and panicking out of her mind. She gave me the horrific news that our sister Dawn had been shot. I nearly dropped the phone. I couldn't believe my ears. Brigette forced the tough words through her emotions and told me that Dawn's children had also been shot. My heart sunk. I was speechless. Something in Brigette's voice made me realize that something even worse had happened. Brigette couldn't bring herself to tell me the entire story.

"Meet us at Mom's house," Brigette cried. "We are all meeting there."

When Brigette hung up the phone a rush of emotions hit me. I felt empty knowing that something terrible had happened to my sister Dawn and her kids. I desperately searched for Henry and finally found him on the street. When my brother got in my truck I had to break the devastating news to him. Henry couldn't believe it. I sped off and made my way to Maryland to find out what happened to my sister. I turned on the radio to see if we could get more news. I turned the dial to WTOP FM and we heard the news flash about my sister. *"There is more news coming up about the quadruple murder at a home in Riverdale, Maryland."* Henry and I fell into a state of shock. Learning that our sister had been murdered sent us into an emotional tailspin. I couldn't believe that my sister Dawn was a homicide victim along with two of her children. We needed to get to Dawn's house and we needed to get there fast. As we arrived we noticed that the P.G. County Police had already blocked off the entire street. No matter how much we pleaded they would not let us anywhere near my sister's home. The entire area had become a crime scene. Henry and I went to my mother's house. Relatives started gathering as the tragic news circulated throughout the family. My mother knew that Dawn and her grandchildren were gone. Their awful passing ate her up inside. My heart ached for her. I knew I had to be strong for my mother. My sister Dawn was a good person. She didn't deserve to be gunned down the way she was in cold blood.

The entire day at my mother's house was filled with tears, memories and questions. No one knew why something so tragic could happen to our family. Everyone knew that my sister Dawn was involved with drugs. Suffering such a brutal ending was something we never thought could happen. As the investigation into the murders commenced, a lot of details began to emerge about that fateful morning.

In 2010, Dawn and her children were sharing a home with her boyfriend's sister. Somehow they got mixed up with a dangerous drug dealer from Texas. The man stashed a large quantity of marijuana at my sister Dawn's house. When the drugs came up missing things took a deadly turn. The big time drug dealer blamed Dawn and her boyfriend's sister. He came to my sister's house with another woman and all hell broke loose. My sister Dawn, her children and her boyfriend's sister were all held at gunpoint. The drug dealer interrogated them but the drugs were never found. In a move of desperation, the cold-hearted criminal decided to end my sister's life and the innocent lives of her two children. Everyone in the house was viciously murdered.

The news of the heinous crime sent shockwaves throughout the state of Maryland. Dawn's tragic story was even covered by CNN. My family could not believe that we had lost Dawn. It was a reality too dark to accept. Two days later, Dawn's body and the bodies of her five-year old son and her two-year old daughter were released to a funeral home in the area. I wanted to see them. I had to see my sister with my own eyes to make sure that she had indeed been killed. Everything in me could not accept the fact that she was gone. My sister Brigette and I drove to the funeral home. The funeral director told us that he would normally deny any requests to view the bodies before they were prepared for the funeral. However, he recognized the pain that our family felt. He agreed to let us see Dawn and her two children.

No words can describe the empty feeling of viewing your loved ones in a body bag. My sister Brigette and I cried the second we recognized Dawn and her children. Her bullet wounds were still visible. Looking at the aftermath of the immense brutality was heartbreaking. I needed to see my sister that day. I couldn't believe someone could take her away from us. Seeing Dawn in a plastic body bag really hit home with me. I could no longer deny the reality that we had lost Dawn and she would be gone forever.

Nearly a week after the killings, the suspects were in custody. We learned more details about the drug dealer and his motives to carry out the quadruple murder. The killer and his accomplice stood trial the following year. My family attended every court date. We sat just a few feet from the man who had murdered Dawn and her children. We viewed the crime scene photos. Blood was everywhere. Viewing the pictures of the bullet riddled bodies was extremely tough. There was rarely a dry eye in the courtroom. My mother took the entire trial very hard. I could never imagine how much pain she felt losing her youngest child and her grandchildren to such a horrific act.

In 2014, nearly four years after the slayings, the State of Maryland found the shooter guilty of four counts of first degree murder. Prosecutors were prepared to pursue the death penalty but the state outlawed the practice before the sentencing phase of the trial. The killer was sentenced to four life sentences without the possibility of parole. His accomplice was sentence to one life term. The shooter will spend the rest of his life behind the walls of a maximum security prison. He will never see the light of day again.

Every year without Dawn has been tough for our family. She died on August 6th which is the same day as my daughter's birthday. For almost three years we were unable to celebrate Solina's birthday. The grieving process had been very hard for us. One year my mother decided that we needed to turn our attention to her granddaughter Solina. My mother told us that it wasn't fair to Solina that we didn't celebrate with her. Solina always loved to celebrate her birthday and my mother made sure that she had a special one. We went over to her house and had a small party for her. Despite the tragedy, it was important to my mother that we continued to celebrate life.

Dealing with the passing of my sister has never gotten easier. Sometimes I think back to the last day I saw her alive. She was on the National Mall working as a tour guide. I was driving near her post and she recognized my vehicle. She waved at me and we spoke briefly. Dawn was always proud of her older brother—the comedian. She gave me the most beautiful smile that day. I never imagined that it would be the last time that I would see her alive.

Over the years I have felt guilty about losing Dawn. I regretted not becoming a larger star and making tons of money. For the longest time, I believed that Dawn would still be alive today if I was more successful as an entertainer. It's possible that I would have been able to help Dawn have a better life. However, no amount of money would guarantee that my sister would have avoided a dangerous lifestyle and not become wrapped up in the drug world.

My brother Henry has also battled with the guilt of losing my baby sister. He lived with Dawn a few nights per week and normally he would have been in the house when the murders occurred. The evening before the tragedy, Henry went into a store in Washington, DC. He bumped into a friend and they started talking. The conversation went on for some time and Henry missed the last bus to Maryland. He decided to sleep on the street that night and wasn't with my sister when everything went down. Henry continues to beat himself up for not being in Maryland. He believes that he would have been able to protect my sister if he was in the house. I believe differently. The killer was with his girlfriend and both assailants were armed. I believe that they were prepared to kill anyone in the house over the drugs.

Although it didn't completely heal us, the successful prosecution and incarceration of Dawn's killer has given our family some closure. Dawn's beautiful life was snatched from her at the early age of thirty-eight years young. Despite her problems and her drug battles, Dawn was always giving and loving. Dawn knew that I was a serious health nut. She knew that I loved anything healthy. About two weeks before she died, Dawn gave me a bottle of green-tea lotion. I had never tried it before and I thought it was a thoughtful gift from my younger sister. I never got a chance to use the lotion. After Dawn lost her life I decided to never crack the seal on the packaging. When I moved to New York I decided to take it with me. I still have the lotion on my bathroom shelf. Sometimes when I miss my sister I hold onto the lotion. I know her DNA is still on the bottle and I can still feel her presence. I speak to Dawn quite often. Whenever I am about to go on stage for a big show I speak to her and reminisce about her life.

My family will never get over the violent end to my sister's life. The tragedy has pulled us closer together. We have always been a tight knit family. We'll always continue to comfort each other as we keep Dawn's memory alive. My brother Henry was dramatically affected by the death of our baby sister. Shortly after we laid Dawn to rest, Henry started to change his life. He shied away from the drugs more and more every day. He eventually kicked the habit and cleaned up his life. He met an amazing woman and they moved into an apartment together. I believe the reality of drug abuse really hit too close to home for Henry once we lost our baby sister. Some tragedies are unavoidable. Sometimes we don't understand why some of the worse things happen to some of the best people. The heavy pain of losing her has never gone away, but I know deep down inside that my sister Dawn is in a better place.

Chapter 20

Catherine Tobias

When people ask me why I started doing magic and comedy they often expect me to give an elaborate response. Most people wait for a large cosmic-style answer that should involve grandiose accolades. My true motivation for studying long hours did not involve a plan to conquer the comedy world. I didn't travel around the globe just to be compared to great magicians of the past and present. I didn't network with hundreds of agents, club owners and managers to simply have people recognize me in public. The root of my true motivation comes down to one person. My beautiful mother.

Everything that I've ever done to further my career has been done for my mom. Even during the early years when I was becoming familiar with the art, I would do everything to please her and make her smile. Once I realized that I could make money in this industry, the hunger to take care of my mother only intensified. My life's plan has always been simple. Keep working and make it big so that my mother didn't have to want for anything.

When people see Catherine Tobias and I together they always recognize that we look alike. If you put a wig on me, I'll look exactly like my mother. I've also been told that I walk just like my mother. Over the years I have picked up a lot of traits from her...both good and bad. I get my outgoing nature from my mother. I get my good looks from my mother. And I also get my sense of humor from my mother. Catherine is the funniest person in our family. She is always the life of the party. She always had the gift of commanding attention in a crowded room. Even now in her golden years, if you have a party you can expect that she'll be dancing not long after she arrives. She will get the party started. My mother might even bust a split in the middle of the dance floor. She loves to have fun.

I have nicknamed my mother "The Black Lucille Ball." She reminds me of the main character from *I Love Lucy* which was an iconic television show in the 1950s. During the show, Lucy was always up to something. She was always sneaky and always in trouble. She was playfully conniving and secretly doing something she shouldn't be doing. Without a doubt, that is my mother. She's The Black Lucille Ball.

My mother has always been a good mom. She raised all her children to love, respect and support each other. My siblings and I are still very close today because of my mother. She taught us how to be a family. When it comes to my career there is no bigger fan than my mom. She will talk your ear off about her son Kevin Lee, the magician and comedian. She could be in a nail salon, a restaurant or even at church and she will bring my name up. She talks about me everywhere she goes. I don't mind a bit. It's good to know that she is proud of me and that she has full confidence in me and my career. When I was younger that wasn't always the case.

"Why don't you get a job?"

I can't count how many times I heard this question in my lifetime. My mother was always concerned that I was putting all of my eggs in one basket. Like all mothers who care for her children, Catherine didn't want me to struggle through life. She would ask me if I was looking for work or if I was considering a job. I would always tell her that I wanted to focus on my career and I had no plans of getting a 9-to-5. I thought I had to change my name to "*why don't you get a job*" because my mother would say that more than she would say my name.

Despite her best intentions, the message would annoy me constantly. Even when my career began to flourish my mother would ask me about a job. It's not uncommon for a person's family to be skeptical about their chances of making it in the entertainment industry. It's a very competitive field and you must be cut from a different cloth to make it. I never once doubted that I had the chops to make some noise in this business. I knew that I would make it to the big stages. I was just unsure of my timeline.

My mother could never understand my passion for success in this business. She could never grasp the concept that everyone had to start somewhere. One day I read a quote from Eddie Murphy. He was speaking about his mother and how she once told him to get a job so that he wouldn't have to struggle. Eddie noted the irony of the conversation he had with his mom. At the time he was working for Saturday Night Live and making nearly $18,000 per week. When I read the quote I immediately thought of my mother.

When I was younger my mother wouldn't come right out and say that she didn't believe in my vision. But I could feel that she was concerned for my future. What my mother didn't know was that everything was going to take a back seat to my dreams. My schooling, my friends, the girls and any thoughts of a job was going to take a backseat to my goals. Becoming a big entertainer had become a part of my fabric and no amount of advice was going to change that. Deep down inside I wanted to make my mother happy, so I was determined to win at all cost.

Throughout my career my determination to succeed has never waned. The entertainment industry is filled with extreme highs and extreme lows. I have been lucky enough to experience both sides. As my career began to blossom it felt good to show my family the results of all my hard work and sacrifice. When I appeared on "*Showtime at the Apollo*" I remember how my mother congratulated me on the accomplishment. Seeing her son on the world famous Apollo stage was a surreal experience for her. I knew she was proud of me.

Nothing in my life gave me more joy then taking my mother to a show to watch me perform. She has seen me in some fantastic venues as a headliner. She's also seen me as the opening act to a number of famous artists. The proudest moment in my career came when I invited my mother out to see me perform at *The Carter Barron*

Amphitheatre to open up for musical legend Gladys Knight. Looking out into the audience and seeing my mother sitting next to Radio One's CEO Cathy Hughes, and watching me perform my set was such a humbling experience. It was a dream-come-true for me. All I ever wanted to do was have my mother right there as thousands of people laughed and cheered at my show. It was a night I will never forget.

As my career grew I was also able to spoil my mother with gifts when I could. One evening I took her to see musical icon Diana Ross in New York City. My mother loved the show. When I was not taking my mother to concerts and events I would buy her all sorts of gifts. I remember buying my mother a mink coat and fancy jewelry. When Christmas came around I made sure it was special for her. I would get her all types of electronics. I even purchased a big screen television for her. She deserved it for being such a great mom to me and my siblings.

Through my networking and constant grinding I managed to get invited to be on a radio show with Cathy Hughes. Her radio station was catching fire at the time and she was hosting a show from her studio on 8th Street in Northwest Washington D.C. I was invited to be a guest alongside the late-great Dick Gregory. The show was an amazing experience and Cathy and I became friends. I introduced her to my mother and they hit it off. They exchanged numbers and my mother would call Cathy Hughes all the time. When tragedy hit my family, Cathy Hughes even reached out to my mother to help in any way she could. My mother's friendship with Cathy Hughes crystallizes my mother's personality. She is such a great person and anyone that crosses her path is immediately drawn into her amazing spirit.

When I think about my mother I can say that she wants nothing but the best for her family. Even when we were children, my mother did everything she could to make sure her kids were straight. My mother was young when she had us, and like all young mothers, she made her share of mistakes. When my mom left my father she made sure that she became acquainted with a man who was all about her kids. My mother never dealt with any man who treated us bad or neglected us. She only introduced good men into our lives, and she always put her family first.

My mother instilled those same principles in her children. She always reminded us that nothing comes before family. When I found out that I had a daughter in the world and I couldn't find her, it was my mother who stayed on me to keep searching.

"Did you find that girl?" My mother would ask when I visited the house. "Did you find Solina?"

I have to credit my mother with staying on me about finding my daughter. She kept me motivated and let me know how important it was for my daughter to have her father in her life. She never let me forget.

When I finally tracked down Solina, it quickly became apparent that I would need a lot of help. My mother did everything she could to assist me. When it was time for me to head out for a tour, my mother was right there to watch Solina for me. My mother was there when Solina was in the marching band. When I couldn't take Solina to her practices, my mother was right there. My mother had to attend all of the parent-teacher meetings to discuss my daughter's progress. During my daughter's competitions and activities, my mother had to step in because I was somewhere in another state working on my career. When I couldn't be there for my daughter, my mother never hesitated to do what needed to be done. Without my mother, Solina wouldn't have been able to do a lot of things. One year I remember there was a Mother-Daughter dinner at her school. Solina's real mother wasn't in the picture, so my mother volunteered to take my daughter to the dinner. My mother has always been a major support for me and Solina. There is no way that my daughter would be the person she is today without her grandmother.

When my career hit a dry spell, the strong relationship I had with my mother began to be tested. I was struggling financially for years due to the inconsistent nature of the business. I would go weeks and sometimes months without a substantial income. It became very difficult to wait around for a major tour or project to bring me back from the financial abyss. In addition to my terrible spending habits I was having a tough time raising my daughter and giving her a good life. Sometimes it felt like we were trapped in a terrible cycle of Ramen-Noodle dinners, shut-off notices and evictions. Things were so bad that I had to move back into my mother's house with my daughter in tow.

No matter how bad things got in my life, I never gave up. I could hear my mother's voice in the back of my head telling me to get a job. I knew she had grown frustrated with my situation and we began to bump heads. To bring in extra income I continued to perform on the streets and juggle for tourists on the National Mall in downtown Washington, D.C. From the outside looking into my life, my mother believed that I was wasting time with my street performing. I tried to explain to her that I was making really good money on the street, but she didn't believe me. We battled all the time about her wanting me to get a job. I told her that I would never get a job at K-Mart or any other low paying location because I was making more than the manager at those companies. Despite our disagreements my mother never let up on me. She just wanted the best for her son and her granddaughter.

It would take years for my mother to finally come around and grasp the full idea of her son being an entertainer. The business has always been a game of 50/50 chance. Hard work and determination doesn't always translate into a successful career. There is some luck and timing that's involved that could determine if you will take the leap from starving-artist to the multi-million dollar status. Even when some entertainers get their big break, there is no guarantee that they will stay on top for long. Making the type of money that could rival a retirement account is no easy feat. What my mother never understood was that I accepted the risk before I started. Never giving up and trying until I succeeded was something that I signed up for. No amount of convincing was ever going to change my mind.

Money was not the only thing that my mother and I disagreed

about. The only time I truly felt disappointed in my mother was during the times in which I divorced my wives. No matter the circumstance of why we chose to part ways, my mother would always side with my ex-wives. It seemed like my mother would never take my side of the argument. I don't know if my mother viewed me as the troublemaker in my marriages, but I always felt like she never valued my side of the story. I never confronted my mother about it. I tried to make sense of it for the longest time. I thought back to the days of the loud arguments that my mother and father would have. I remember her being very upset and talking to my father like a dog. She would curse him out with no remorse. My dad's mother would always stick up for him. My grandmother Ruth didn't want anyone speaking bad about her son. But my mother was not like that when it came to me. Whenever there was a fight or disagreement in my marriages my mother would always side with the women. The disagreements we had over my finances paled in comparison to how my mother disappointed me by never sticking up for me during those rough times with my ex-wives.

I know my mother is not perfect. And neither are her kids. I believe we all tried our hardest to make our parents proud. My mother is a strong woman. She takes on everyone else's problems as if they were her own. I know she carries unnecessary stress with her and she tends to worry about things she has no control of. I'm happy that we live in the social media age today. My mother can finally see all the success that surrounds her son. She can now follow me and see that things are a lot better today than they were for me yesterday.

When I was younger I told myself that I was going to buy my mother a million-dollar home. I gave myself a deadline. By the time I turned twenty-eight years of age, I wanted to buy my mother that house. Unfortunately, I missed that mark by a few years and my mother never got the home. But I have never given up on the dream. I still push hard to turn my name into a household brand. I still work nonstop for my mother and I want her to always be proud of her son. We have had our battles over the years. When it was time to finish high school, I rebelled and decided to chase my passion. I also rebelled when it came time to look for work. I knew I had to stay the course. Everything I've done in my career is dedicated to my mother. I wouldn't trade her for anyone else on the planet. We both have made mistakes in our lives and I have forgiven her for everything. The good mom in her has always outweighed the bad mom. When I think of the things she has given me, I could never thank her enough. Of all the traits that I picked up from my mother over the years, one trait stands out. The motivation she passed on to me keeps the fire burning inside of me. I wake up every morning with the motivation to do well for her because that is how much I love her.

Chapter 21

A Divine Reunion

People come into your life for a reason, a season, or a lifetime. When I think back on my experiences, I am always amazed by the number of remarkable fans and supportive friends who have made me a better entertainer and more importantly, a better man. I've crossed paths with thousands of people during my career. Some people have become a blur in my memory, and some people will forever be etched in my heart.

During my early years as an entertainer, I was booked to work a comedy club in Poughkeepsie, New York. I was still getting my feet wet as a traveling comedian, so it was exciting to hop in my hooptie and take the six-hour drive to upstate New York to perform. When I arrived in New York, I was introduced to the manager of the club. She was one of the most beautiful girls I had ever seen. She was a former model who was recruited by the club owner to manage his venue. I was immediately attracted to her. She told me her name was Patricia. I introduced myself and it didn't take long for us to hit it off.

For the next few months Patricia and I engaged in a long-distance relationship. Mobile phones were not popular back in those days so we had to communicate through beepers and landlines. We even wrote letters to each other. When I was booked to work in the New York area I would make it my business to see Patricia. She would come to my shows to support me, and we would hang out whenever we could. It was hard to maintain our relationship. My career was steadily growing which made traveling back and forth to the New York area extremely difficult. We were both very busy and our friendship suffered from it. When I decided to take the big leap and head out to California, my friendship with Patricia became a casualty as well. We sent photos and letters to each other to keep the fire burning. But after a while it became impossible for us to continue our long distance relationship and we lost total contact with each other.

About twenty years and two divorces later, I reconnected with Patricia through a mutual friend on Facebook. Patricia told me that she was still in the Poughkeepsie area and she was still managed the *Bananas Comedy Club*. I was extremely happy to hear from her. She suggested adding me to an upcoming comedy show and of course I agreed. She made a call to the owner, Holland Jameson, and set everything up. I was excited about the news because I wanted to see my friend again. A few weeks later I was on the road and making the six-hour ride to the comedy club. When I got to the venue I saw Patricia standing at the front entrance. It was love at first sight all over again. We greeted one other and it was like we were never apart. It felt like we hadn't missed a beat.

I went on stage that night and had a great show. After the event Patricia and I headed out for a late-night dinner. We sat down and caught up for hours. I filled her in on everything that I had been going through in my career. I told her about the *Def Comedy Jam* days and working on the road with Sinbad. I told her about my California trips and also raising my beautiful daughter Solina. Patricia filled me in on her life as well. Managing the comedy club was a wild ride for her. She told me about all of the now famous comedians that came through the comedy club up in Poughkeepsie.

Patricia told me about the night Jimmy Fallon came to the *Bananas Comedy Club*. Jimmy was a rising comic back then and he was a contestant in a comedy competition hosted by the comedy club. Jimmy placed first place in the competition and his career began to skyrocket from that event. Patricia has always taken pride in being the person who helped put Jimmy Fallon on the stage that evening at the *Bananas Comedy Club*. Patricia also told me about how Chris Rock was a regular at the club. She also mentioned names like Sinbad and Tommy Davidson as prior guests on the Bananas stage. She told me all about the exciting nights in Poughkeepsie and I was happy to hear that she was having fun and flourishing at the club.

As the night went on, we began to talk about our personal lives. I was in a relationship at the time and Patricia was dealing with a cheating husband. It was hard for us to deny the attraction we still had for each other. The old feelings that burned in us began to rekindle and the affair began. We would meet in hotels in and around the New Jersey area. We had to keep our love a secret because the club owners of the *Bananas Comedy Club* treated Patricia like a daughter and didn't want Patricia to get hurt. We feared that they would try to break us up if we were ever found out, so we never publicized our affair. Once Patricia finally divorced her husband we told the owners about our relationship and they gave us their blessings.

When I reconnected with Patricia my career was in a tough place. I was still a traveling comedian but I wasn't working enough to maintain my double life as a father and an entertainer. I needed to be more productive and I just couldn't find the time nor the energy to manage my household and my career. My daughter Solina was in her teenage years at the time. I was a very strict father and also paranoid about her future. She was starting to date boys and was experimenting with sex, and it was driving me crazy. I was worried that she would become a young mother and ruin her chances of having a great life. All I ever wanted for my daughter was for her to get good grades and head off to college. I never wanted her to be like thousands of young girls her age that hung around the wrong people and made life-altering mistakes. Solina and I would clash all the time and it was putting a strain on our father-daughter relationship.

After Patricia separated from her husband our feelings for each other became public. We openly hung out a lot more and our feelings only grew stronger. Patricia would visit me more often in Maryland and she finally got a chance to meet Solina. They instantly hit it off. I was happy that Patricia and my daughter had a great connection. In the past I have brought dozens of women around Solina. That is something I regret. My daughter longed to have a mother in her life.

When I would bring my female friends back to our apartment, Solina would always ask me if the woman was her new mommy. It broke my heart to tell her no. I later realized that Solina needed a connection that I could never fulfill. She needed the love and support of a mother figure.

With Patricia now in my life things began to change. She and Solina started to have a great connection and that made me happy. Solina was more mature at this point and was slowly becoming a young woman. Patricia helped a lot with giving her the guidance and wisdom that only a female could pass on to one another. Over the years their relationship continued to get stronger. From the start it seemed like their connection was something that could only be described as divine.

On August 6, 1993, Patricia was eight months pregnant. An incident occurred that evening that forced her to be rushed to the emergency room. The doctors on staff had to perform an emergency surgery to save her life and the life of her baby. During the procedure Patricia suffered from placenta previa which caused her to have internal bleeding. The surgeons scrambled to limit the damage. Patricia lived through the horrifying event but tragically her unborn child did not survive. Around the same time that Patricia was battling for her life, another woman I was connected to was in the hospital. My daughter's mother, Venus, was giving birth in a hospital down in Virginia. On August 6, 1993 my daughter Solina was born.

It has always been hard for me to ignore the significance of those two events happening on the same day. Once we reconnected and I revealed my daughter's birthday to her, Patricia's eyes grew wide as saucers. She told me the story about her brush with death on that very same day. I was heartbroken about the news but I realized then that there had to be a divine reason that helped us to reconnect after so many years.

Connecting with my daughter was only one piece to Patricia's influence on my new life. Patricia came in and saved my career. I mean that in the most literal sense possible. The entertainment business has always been rough. It's a tight business and you must be on your job if you want to succeed. Keeping a lucrative tour schedule and raising my daughter had begun to take a toll on my career. It became nearly impossible to keep up with it all. Patricia came in and helped me get organized. Working at the *Bananas Comedy Club* had given her decades of experience in the world of entertainment. Her management skills were key to putting my career back on track. Patricia became my manager. She made the calls that I couldn't make and helped to negotiate more gigs for me. We did a major overhaul of my social media and made sure that my website was updated. We managed to distribute my promo videos through various digital outlets and targeted dozens of booking agents and club owners. Patricia removed a large burden from my shoulders. While she assisted me with the business side of things, I was free to work on my stage act.

As our relationship grew, Patricia and I decided to become business partners. She was still working at the *Bananas Comedy Club* which was now under new ownership. The previous owner Holland Jameson sold the club to another person. Mr. Jameson didn't sell the club to Patricia because he felt that the venue was losing too much money and it would eventually fail. Patricia continued to work for the new owner. He relied on her to keep the business afloat. Patricia would put in long hours at the club and make sure everything ran smooth. Once I learned of her compensation every week I was not happy. I knew Patricia was helping to make his business grow. The club was profitable yet Patricia wasn't getting paid what she deserved. We began to discuss the possibility of starting our own comedy club. Patricia knew the business like the back of her hand so we felt it would be a great investment for us. As fate would have it, the venue that hosted the comedy club lost its liquor license. The comedy nights had to be closed down. Patricia and I approached a friend of hers with the idea. They agreed to partner with us and less than a year later we opened up Carmine's Comedy Club in Poughkeepsie, New York.

When I was a young comedian paying my dues throughout the comedy circuit, I never dreamed of owning my own venue. In fact, I would have never imaged that my first comedy club would be in New York. I was told on numerous occasions that New York clubs would never touch me with a ten-foot pole because I was a so-called prop comic. To have a flourishing comedy club in New York brings me enormous joy. It always feels good to silence the naysayers and prove to people that anything is possible with hard work and determination. Thanks to Patricia we have one of the busiest comedy clubs in the region and all of our sacrifices were worth it.

From helping me organize my business, to giving my daughter another positive role model, Patricia has been a special addition to my life. I always say that Patricia was a gift because we reconnected at the perfect time. I could never repay her for giving my career a special breath of fresh air. She gave me the energy, organization and motivation I needed to fight through those tough times. I've since moved from the Maryland area and I am finally in New York. Throughout my career I was given a few opportunities to move up north but I decided against it. The circumstances were not right when I was younger. They say that everything happens for a reason and sometimes your life doesn't move along as planned. I'm finally in a space with the right person to once again reach for the stars and trust the process.

Chapter 22

The World Stage

My career has taken me to many exotic corners of the globe. When I was a young boy I tried to imagine the feeling of being loved and respected by fans of all nationalities. The sweet realization of my dreams surpassed far beyond my childhood fantasies. My climb hasn't been easy. I've come a long way. I often find myself excited about what the future holds for my family and my career as I continue on this amazing journey. Now that I'm considered a seasoned veteran in the business, younger entertainers ask me for advice whenever they can. The knowledge and the lessons that I have acquired over the years have come with many emotional scars. As a student of the arts, I know how important it is to gain wisdom from afar. Every minute in this game will bring new opportunities to learn and grow. For anyone looking to break into the business it is essential to keep an open mind. To create a sustainable career it is always wise to learn as much as you can, as fast as you can. This helps to keep pace with an ever changing industry.

Thinking outside the box is something that I take pride in. When I was an amateur entertainer I made the decision to focus on being different. I always wanted my act to stand out from the rest. Blending comedy with my magic would prove to be the best decision I ever made for my career. My unique act has been able to survive many ups and downs of the industry. I have been able to showcase my set to a wide range of audiences. With a few tweaks I continue to dazzle crowds from the mainstream, urban and international stages. I've seen hundreds of comedians come and go in this industry. The survivors are typically the ones that can adjust their style and seamlessly move in and out of various venues. Of all the lessons I have learned in this business, thinking outside of the box and being different is at the head of the list.

Another lesson I have learned from all of my years in this industry is the importance of maintaining a healthy lifestyle. The Walk of Fame in Hollywood is littered with names of celebrities who left us too soon due to drug addiction and alcohol abuse. I've always managed to stay away from that destructive lifestyle. I've seen firsthand how a beautiful life can spin out of control for anyone that has to battle with addiction. I never wanted my career to suffer as a result of making poor choices. I always made a conscious effort to stay clean, despite the constant temptations that surrounded me.

Maintaining a healthy lifestyle is not only staying away from substance abuse but it also involves taking care of your body. Traveling around the world and consistently bringing a killer show requires a great deal of energy. I am always impressed when I see performers well beyond their fifties that bring more stage presence than their younger counterparts. To perform at a high level every night is no easy feat. Watching your diet is very important. As a traveling comic I often find myself on the highway as I tour from city to city. It is hard to find healthy choices from the rest areas and truck stops. I do my best to avoid damaging foods and beverages that will slow me down. I have witnessed too many fellow comics and entertainers who were forced to cut their careers short due to health issues. No matter where my journey leads me in this industry, I will always make a healthy lifestyle my priority.

As an African-American entertainer who is constantly on the road, finding healthy places to eat is often the least of my problems. I learned early in my career to be extremely careful as I traveled from state to state to do my shows. I can't count the number of times that I have been pulled over by police officers in various states. Some officers were professional and courteous to me. However, there were a number of incidents when I sensed that I was being harassed because of the color of my skin. Racial profiling is very real in the United

States and has been for many decades. The practice of pulling over motorists because of their race happens every day on our highways. As a traveling comic I had become victimized by that practice many times. Having New York license plates and traveling to a small town made me a target for overzealous cops looking to abuse their power.

One evening I was traveling to a comedy show in a small town in Alabama. It was a cold night and I was looking forward to having an amazing show. Before I reached my hotel I was pulled over by two police officers who were looking to investigate why I was in the area. The officers approached my car and asked me to exit my vehicle. I got out and stood a few feet from my car. One of the officers proceeded to illegally conduct a search of my person. He never told me the reason for the search. I was too afraid to argue with a pair of Alabama officers on the side of the road. As the cop patted me down he grazed over my groin and looked at me.

"Is that your package?" The cop aggressively asked.

I was confused by the question. I didn't know what to say so I decided to respond with the first thing that came to mind.

"Yes, that is my package," I uttered.

The mood of the officers changed. I could tell that they were alarmed and one of the cops told me to pull down my pants. I couldn't believe the order. The officers were dead serious. I didn't want things to spin out of control so I decided to comply. I pulled down my pants on the side of the road.

"Where's your package?" The cop snapped at me.

Again, I was confused. I looked down and pointed at my penis.

"Well, you're looking at it," I responded.

The officers were not amused. I didn't realize it at the time but the cops assumed that I was carrying drugs in my underwear. Needless to say that I was no trafficker and this was not a drug bust. The officer ordered me to pull my pants up. He was clearly upset. The officers let me go with a warning and I never received a ticket for the traffic stop.

As I spent more time on the road and the traffic stops continued, I decided to travel with a lot of promotional materials. Even today

I travel with my headshots and media articles that identify me as a professional entertainer. Any time I am pulled over by an officer, I make it a point to state my business in the area. Sometimes it is a hassle to be delayed in my travels, but I have found it useful to be very cooperative and forthcoming to avoid any misunderstandings.

The highway is not the only place where I have experienced racism throughout my travels. As an African American comedian, dealing with racist hecklers has also been a part of my experience. I have been called a *Nigger* on stage by a drunken white woman who was eventually thrown out the club. I was shocked by the outburst but it wasn't the last time. One evening I wore a t-shirt for a late comedian who I had admired. Richard Pryor had recently passed away and I wanted to pay tribute to him. In the middle of my set someone from the audience screamed out, *"Who is that Nigger on your shirt?"* Again the heckler was removed from the club.

I never let the racism on stage get to me. Even when I was called a *Nigger* by a former agent, I didn't let it faze me. In this business you must have thick skin. Everyone will not be nice and polite to you. Learning how to properly handle rude and difficult people is part of the business. In the world of entertainment there are a lot of politics. Most of the rules are unwritten. As a young comic I had to learn many lessons the hard way. Dealing with total strangers who insulted me and wished me ill has always been disappointing. But nothing was more difficult to handle than the feeling of being wronged by a person I considered my friend.

Before the television appearances and international tours I was good friends with a fellow comedian from the Washington, D.C. area. Like a lot of struggling entertainers back in the late eighties, we performed together at small clubs and dreamed about one day making it big. My good friend was very talented. We both were confident that we were going to be huge stars in the business. If we were not playing basketball together or traveling to different comedy clubs, my good friend and I were constantly talking about how we could make a breakthrough in the business. One day my friend and I were traveling to Solomon's Island, Maryland. We were scheduled to perform that evening at a small comedy club. I believe we were making roughly two hundred dollars between the two of us. I was riding in his blue Ford Escort and as always, we were discussing the industry.

"I'll make a deal with you," my good friend said as he drove closer to our destination.

"Okay. What's that?" I asked.

"Whoever makes it big first has to come back and help the next person up." He said.

He reached out his hand and we shook on the deal. It made a lot of sense that we would make the success-pact together. We were both pushing hard to be successful and we knew that it was just a matter of time before one of us struck it big. Our handshake solidified the deal and we promised that we would pull each other up when the time came.

As fate would have it, our deal never panned out. My good friend went on to explode into a mega star. He moved to Los Angeles and made himself into a household name. Unfortunately, my good friend has never made good on our handshake. We shared a number of stages after his rise to fame and he never mentioned our deal. He never reached back to assist me, nor offered any help with my career. As my friend became more successful, we eventually lost contact. Over the years it has been a disappointing reality to deal with. I was always proud of my friend's success and excited to see him do well. But as the years flew by with no contact I realized that a helping hand from my good friend would never happen. In the entertainment industry it is never a good thing to be bitter. Although I was upset about how things turned out between us, I never let that failed promise change the person I am. There are a lot of moving parts in the industry and success can hinge on a number of factors. Hard work, timing, networking and even luck plays a major part in how far someone can make it in this business. For a friend not to reach back was an eye-opening experience for me. I promised myself that I would never distance myself from a good friend because of my success. I have never broken that promise.

A few years after my good friend moved to California and launched his successful movie career, I became friends with another dynamic young comedian from the D.C. area. We became tight and performed at a few comedy clubs together. The young comedian looked up to me. We hung out a few times and I talked to him about the business. The young comedian often spoke about his plans to move up north. One day he came to me and told me that he had just got an apartment in New York City. He asked me to come up with him and be his roommate. It sounded like a great opportunity and I agreed to make the move with him. I knew that New York was filled with more opportunities than the DMV area so I told the young comedian that I would share the apartment with him.

A few weeks later I changed my mind. I was already an established comic in the area. The idea of moving to another city seemed like too much of a gamble for me. I had an apartment, a car and a gorgeous girlfriend at the time. I didn't want to risk my current situation by closing down shop in Maryland. I decided to forego the move and build on what I had already established in the DMV area.

When I told the young comedian about the change of plans, he was understandably upset. He left the area soon after and moved to New York without me. The young comedian connected with the right people and found himself starring in a movie within the next year. His name spread like wildfire and before long the young comedian was signing a multi-million dollar deal to star in his own sketch-comedy show. His amazing rise was very fast and I was proud of his accomplishments.

I later found out through a mutual friend that the young comedian was still upset that I didn't travel north with him. Later in my career I eventually made my move to New York, but before then the timing didn't seem right. I often think of how different things would have been if I didn't get cold feet. I try not to dwell on missed opportunities in my life but I do understand the importance of reflection. Although I don't fully regret my decision, I have learned a valuable lesson. Some choices in life require a leap of faith. To be successful you have to take risks and trust the process. The key is to follow your heart and not follow the leader. Everyone's journey is different and there are no guarantees in life. It took a few years for me to understand that my road to success was different. Every misstep only motivated me to push harder and excel.

Having close friends turn into celebrities and then turn into strangers is nothing new in the world of entertainment. It is something that happens every day. Of course, having my friends to move on and never reach back was disappointing. I'm only human. To say that I wasn't hurt by how things turned out would be disingenuous. Losing close friends is never easy. But the wisdom gained from those unfortunate events is priceless.

As I became more successful in my own career my circle of friends has only grown stronger. I am still close with my best friend Fat Doctor and we speak on a regular basis. My cousin Dennis, who was my magician's assistance when I was just a pre-teen, is also still in my life. Dennis was instrumental in helping me land a major tour gig with one of the most successful jazz musicians of our generation. In 2004, I toured with the legendary Wynton Marsalis. The nine-time Grammy Award winner invited me on the road for The Magic Hour Tour. My cousin Dennis was Wynton's tour manager at the time and he came up with the idea to have a magician as an opening act. Wynton agreed and I was added to the nationwide tour.

Being on the road with Wynton was nothing short of amazing. The tour covered dozens of venues as we traveled from New York City to the west coast. No matter where the tour bus stopped, Wynton Marsalis was well received. People loved him. He was like the Michael Jackson of the jazz world. Local fans, fellow musicians and A-List celebrities would all come out to watch Wynton and his band play. To open up for Wynton was an honor. I performed in front of some great crowds. People loved my act everywhere we went. Wynton's fans were loyal and every event was sold out. Even after the show people wanted to be around Wynton and his crew. I remember a few occasions when we visited the home of some of Wynton's wealthy friends and fans. It seemed like every other night we were being invited to hang out at somebody's mansion in the area. It was such a remarkable time.

Although Wynton has countless celebrity friends, he has always been a down to earth person. He has never let his world-renowned success go to his head. We have had many conversations about life and the industry. I learned a lot from Wynton. He was never afraid to speak his mind and express his beliefs. I admired that about him. One evening while we were driving through Albuquerque, New Mexico on the tour bus, a few of us were discussing basketball. Wynton joined the conversation and started to brag about his basketball skills. In less than five minutes the entire bus was in an uproar. All of us were talking smack to each other and chirping about our skills.

Wynton got hyped and yelled at the bus driver. "Find me a basketball court right now!"

We were all laughing but Wynton was serious. Wynton took a lot of pride in his basketball skills and he was motivated to school us. The bus driver drove around Albuquerque until he found an outdoor basketball court. We all grabbed our tennis shoes and unloaded off the tour bus. It didn't take long for a full blown basketball game to break out. We were all out there balling hard and trying to show each other up. If it wasn't for the fact that we had a performance in just a few hours, it is very possible that we would have been playing basketball with Wynton all night.

That's exactly how Wynton was. He's the genuine article. One minute he would be performing in front of a sold-out crowd for thousands of people and later that night we would see him having a jam session in a local jazz club for thirty people. For a man with all of his accomplishments, Wynton was always personable. While we were out on the road we received the unfortunate call that Ray Charles had passed away. The news devastated all of us. Wynton Marsalis was asked to play at the funeral and he accepted. We took a break from the tour and drove up to Los Angeles to pay our respect to the legend. Watching Wynton move heaven and earth to say goodbye to Ray Charles was a testament to Wynton's character.

Even after I finished the tour, Wynton Marsalis and my cousin Dennis remained close. Wynton is always supportive of the Lee family. When my mother lost her parents on two separate occasions, Wynton Marsalis came to the funerals to pay his respects. He is a prime example of how a person can be a celebrity and possess amazing humility.

The entertainment industry is filled with people from all walks of life. Money and fame doesn't make the person. It only magnifies who they already are. To any young entertainer looking to make a splash in the business my advice would be simple. Find out who you are and never let the ups and downs of the business sway you to be untrue to yourself.

Chapter 23

Wanda Sykes

L ife lessons come in various forms. The old phrase "you learn something new every day" has applied to me throughout my life. My career path has always been filled with great times, high-pressure moments and amazing people that have taught me lessons that could last me ten lifetimes. I look back on some of the friends that have rotated in and out of my life and I'm always surprised at how things turned out. Some people that I've considered friends have disappointed me. And strangers have come into my life and uplifted me. The rise to stardom will expose the true spirit of people. I've been a witness to both the ugly and beautiful sides of the business.

As a young comic working throughout the Maryland, Virginia and Washington, D.C. area, I've been blessed to share the stage with some of the most amazing stand-up talent that this country has ever seen. We all fought and scrambled for stage time as we pushed nonstop to get our names out to the mainstream. Some of us became friends that later grew apart while some comics I barely knew back then became some of my closest friends. It's funny how life plays itself out sometimes.

During my early professional years in the late 80's I worked the comedy circuit in the greater DMV area. I was already a few years ahead of many of the young comics so I was constantly booked as the headliner. During one of my sets, a young female comedian named Wanda Sykes opened up for me. She was from Portsmouth, Virginia and she traveled north a lot to gain more exposure for her act. When I met Wanda she was very down to earth and not afraid of the microphone. She didn't have a lot of material in those days but she

223

was very funny. After a few shows in the area it was clear that she had a knack for comedy.

Wanda became the opening act during a lot of my shows. I was earning about $150 per night and she was making about half of that. Despite the low pay, Wanda and I brought energy every night like we were million-dollar comics. I remember working with Wanda at Andrews Air Force Base and a number of other locations throughout Maryland. One evening we were booked on the same event at a small comedy location called *Griff's Restaurant* in Frederick, Maryland. Wanda met me in the parking lot of the Beltway Plaza Mall in Greenbelt. She hopped in my silver Corvette and we headed up to perform at the small eighty-seat venue. We performed at plenty of locations like Griff's back in those days. Wanda and I talked a lot during those performance nights but we didn't hang out much during the off times. I tried to offer up as much advice as I could about the business and share what I had learned with her. Wanda was always a hard worker and she was serious about her dreams of hitting the big time. After a few years of working the DMV circuit Wanda headed up to New York to try her luck in a larger market.

It didn't take long for Wanda to make a name for herself in the big apple. She made a lot of great connections, including working with a funny comic by the name of Lance Crouther. Before long, Wanda found herself opening up for Chris Rock at *Caroline's Comedy Club* in Times Square. Chris Rock and Wanda became good friends and she began to write for the *Chris Rock Show* on HBO. The show was nominated for numerous Emmy Awards and in 2001, Wanda Sykes won the award for her outstanding writing on the show. Wanda's career skyrocketed.

After Wanda left the Washington, D.C. area we lost contact with each other. As I continued to showcase my act in and out of the country, it was hard not to notice the amazing success that surrounded Wanda and her career. I watched a number of her movies and stand-up specials on television. Her rise in the industry was amazing and well deserved. Wanda had come a long way from working the small comedy clubs in the DMV area to starring in television sitcoms and sitting on the couch with Jay Leno, Conan O'Brien and more. Wanda's story is a true success story.

Wanda and I finally reconnected on social media. We started following each other through Twitter. We congratulated each other on the success that we had found in the industry. By that time Wanda had undoubtedly become a household name and it was cool to reconnect with her.

In 2015, Wanda was tapped to produce Season 8 & 9 of NBC's hit show "*Last Comic Standing*". The show was billed as a competition between some of the best comics in the country. The winner would receive a cash prize of $250,000 and a developmental deal with NBC for a sitcom to be aired on the network. The show had been slumping in ratings so NBC called on Wanda to help make the show a success again. Wanda and I were still communicating through Twitter and Wanda reached out to me and gave me the news. She let me know that she was the Executive Producer of the show and that she thought it would be a good opportunity for me. I was very familiar with the show. I was happy that Wanda was involved and agreed to participate. Wanda didn't show me any favoritism. She informed me that I would have to audition just like everyone else. The show had been marred by controversy in the past, so Wanda wanted to make sure the integrity of the show was always protected. The associated producers scheduled an audition date for me and once again I prepared myself for another big opportunity.

A few weeks later I was in a New York City comedy club. The place was packed to capacity. As I stood backstage and prepared the final touches of my routine, I thought about the fact that I would be auditioning for a chance to be featured on the largest comedy competition in television history. The thought excited me. I had been preparing my entire life for the big stages and I was ready to show the world what I was made of. When I emerged from the curtains the first thing I noticed was that Wanda Sykes was nowhere to be found. A few producers and her partners were front and center but

Wanda wasn't there. From the moment I was introduced I started my act with a bang. The audience loved my show and everyone enjoyed themselves. After my set, the producers told me that a recording of the audition would be mailed back to California and I would hear from them if I was chosen.

A number of weeks went by and I had not heard anything from the producers. I was tempted to reach out to Wanda online but I decided against it. Another week went by and I received an email from the producers stating that they loved my audition tape. They informed me that I was invited to participate in another audition round. This round would determine if I was to make the show. I was thrilled.

A few weeks later I was back in New York and auditioning for the show. When I walked into the venue I noticed a stark difference from the first audition. I had performed for a large audience a few weeks prior but this time I would be asked to audition for just a few people in a performance hall. I noticed three NBC executives in the front row. I quickly looked around for Wanda and noticed she was sitting near the back of the theater in the shadows where I could barely see her.

Most live performers feed off the energy of the audience to put on a great show. As a comedian/magician it is always important to gage the vibe of the crowd to switch gears and timing if the set calls for it. To go on stage and be funny for four people in a large theater is very hard to do for the average comedian. But I never considered myself average. I knew that the audition for *Last Comic Standing* was a huge deal. I made sure to pick out the most amazing outfit for this last round of auditions. I knew that Wanda had not seen me in person in over 20 years and I was determined to make sure that I made a lasting impression before I left the stage. I wanted Wanda and her team to see that I was well prepared for the big stage.

Despite the absence of an audience I had another great set. I felt good about the performance. I knew my timing was flawless and all of my bits fired off without a hitch. Wanda and her team never left their seats. They thanked us all for participating in the auditions. They asked us all to wait for a call to let us know if we had been chosen for the show.

Forty-eight hours later I got the call from NBC. They told me the producers loved my set. I was beyond ecstatic by the news that I would be one of the contestants on the show. I knew I did everything possible to make sure my act was ready for Hollywood. I was finally going to showcase my act again. This time it would be in front of the largest audience I could ever imagine.

The preparation for *Last Coming Standing* was like nothing I had ever experienced. It was not the first time I was on television but dealing with NBC was an entirely different level. NBC presented us with a contract that looked like it was written by one hundred lawyers. In order to be a contestant on the show we had to complete a ton of paperwork. It was nothing like the BET and *Def Comedy Jam* days. There were so many rules and regulations. On HBO, all of the comedians were given free reign over their material. We could do clean jokes, dirty jokes, cocaine jokes, gay jokes and even sex jokes. HBO network encouraged freeform comedy with no restrictions to appeal to an audience that wanted unfiltered content. That was not the case with NBC.

NBC was catering to a mainstream audience during primetime television. We had to be sure not to offend anyone and appeal to a wider audience. NBC also controlled what we wore on the show. We could not wear any clothes with visible logos and the producers had to approve our outfit. I submitted three suits I wanted to wear and the producers chose the one I ultimately wore that evening on television. The strenuous preparation for *Last Comic Standing* made me nervous about the show, but I knew I had to bring my A-game if I wanted to make it far in the competition.

A few weeks before we taped the first episode of the show, Wanda emailed me with some news. She informed me that NBC was interested in doing a background story on me. There was a buzz going around that I would make it far in the show so they wanted to film a segment that would include my family life and more specifically my daughter Solina. I never hesitated to let anyone know that I was a proud father so I immediately agreed to film the segment.

The following week the producers flew me and Solina out to Los Angeles. NBC spared no expense on the trip. We flew to California first class and stayed at the Universal City Hilton Hotel. The producers made sure we were picked up in the finest Town Cars and chauffeured around during our stay. It was an amazing experience to have my daughter with me during this trip. The producers took me and Solina to visit Venice Beach. We talked about my days of street performing just to pay the bills. It was a proud moment to show my daughter how far her father had come and NBC wanted to capture it all for the show. The filming lasted over five hours. We were shadowed by a full camera crew with nearly a half-dozen large studio cameras. NBC spent thousands of dollars to complete my segment. It was a very special day for me and I was happy to share it with my daughter.

About two months later I traveled back to California. The day had finally come for me to perform live on *Last Comic Standing*. I felt good about my chances on the show. I was confident that I had put in the hard work and I was ready for the primetime. I knew that my family would be watching and as always, I wanted to make them proud.

I came out that night and I had a great set. From the moment I hit the stage I felt good about my energy. I was far from nervous or intimidated by the multi-million dollar set or the packed out studio set. My five-minute set was hilarious from the start and I kept the audience laughing. After my set the audience gave me a huge round of applause and now it was time to learn what the judges thought of my act.

The *Last Comic Standing* panel consisted of three judges. Keenen Ivory Wayans and Roseanne Barr were returning from the previous season and Norm Macdonald was brought in to give the panel a sharper bite. Macdonald was hired to be the Simon Cowell of the panel. I knew this would be a tough panel but I was confident I could win them over. The first judge to speak on my performance was Roseanne.

"I absolutely loved you. I can see you on a sitcom," Roseanne said.

The audience clapped and approved of her compliment. The cheers were music to my ears. I thought to myself, *I am on my way.*

The second judge to speak was Keenen Ivory Wayans.

"You remind me of the Crenshaw Clowns," Keenen joked and laughed to himself.

The statement was meant to be an insult. The joke was in reference to two brothers who performed clown shows in the hood. My act was far more superior to a kid's production and Keenen insisted on belittling my act. Any hopes of surviving the show from that point were extinguished. Norm Macdonald piled on with the insults and I was ultimately eliminated from the show. Once again I was forced to deal with the reality that some people just didn't get my act. A black man blending comedy and magic was something that they hadn't seen before. Because they couldn't understand my act, it could not be considered good stand-up in their eyes.

Being eliminated from *Last Comic Standing* was very tough for me. I thought my set was strong enough to get me to the next round. I knew the audience loved my act and I will always hold on to the compliments I got from Roseanne Barr. For the sake of my career I knew I had to pick myself up and keep pushing forward. I didn't hear from Wanda Sykes for nearly a year after my elimination from the show. The segment with my daughter on Venice Beach never aired. I was left with the burning question of what could have been if I would have made it beyond the first round.

In the early part of 2016, I received an email from Wanda. She was working on a tour and her opening act had fallen ill. Wanda asked me if I would be interested in heading out on the road with her. I told her that I would be honored to. Wanda told me that she was reaching out because she considered me to be a part of her inner circle. She didn't trust a lot of people around her. She wanted to tour with somebody she felt comfortable with so she contacted me. I was happy to hear that.

For the better part of the year, Wanda Sykes and I toured throughout the country. We performed in large venues from Chicago to Indianapolis to Atlantic City. Every performance was a sold-out experience. The tour was amazing. I performed for the first time in Las Vegas all because Wanda invited me on the tour. Wanda was already a huge star and the tour only crystallized the love people have for her. Night after night we performed at different venues like we did back in the DMV area. Only this time, I was the opening act and Wanda was making a little bit more than $75 per show. That price would barely get you one ticket.

While we were in Minneapolis, Wanda was speaking to a woman and I overheard her say something that touched me.

"You know Kevin has always been nice to me since I was a young comic," Wanda said.

Her statement made me think back to those nights performing throughout the DMV. I couldn't believe Wanda remembered those days when we were both struggling comedians performing together. It made me realize how special of a person she really is. Wanda has seen a level of success that only a few black female comics can rival. Yet she reached back to assist me with my career. That was something Wanda didn't have to do. She owed me nothing. To message me after nearly two decades and invite me to perform on NBC was nothing short of Wanda being the great person that she is. I can never thank her enough for that. Touring with her and even my brief appearance on *Last Comic Standing* has helped me increase my exposure and build my status.

Wilson Mizner once said that you have to be nice to people on the way up because you'll meet them again on your way down. I have learned that there is no rhyme or reason for the way people act in this business. Time will ultimately show you who your real friends are and who will abandon you if given the opportunity. I'm forever grateful to say that I'm friends with such a sweet, generous and successful woman.

Chapter 24

A Deeper Focus

As any traveling entertainer will confess, taking care of your body is top priority if you want to have a flourishing career on the road. Since a teenager I have been a health fanatic. I've stayed diligent and tried to keep my body in the best shape possible. I try to eat healthy and exercise when I can. Despite my best efforts, I learned a few years ago that health scares are simply unavoidable.

One day back when we were living in our small apartment, my daughter and I were play-fighting. For the longest time, we both shared one important trait. Neither one of us enjoys being tickled. We both knew that about each other so at any given moment a tickle fight would break out between us. Solina would attack me unexpectedly, or I would attack her unexpectedly. The game was simple. If you were caught off guard, you would be tickled mercilessly. On this particular day I had Solina pinned down. I was tickling her armpits, and she was playfully trying to get away from me. As she struggled to break free, she was kicking her legs and she accidently kicked me in the eye. The blow was very painful. She had put all of her strength into it, and it was a really bad kick. At the time, because she was my daughter, I did not want to let her know that I was hurt…but I was really struggling to recover. I didn't want Solina to feel any guilt so I never let her know how badly she hurt me. The pain was excruciating. I put some ice on my eye and nursed it until the swelling went down. I never went to the hospital nor had my eye checked out. A few days later the pain subsided and I never thought anything else of the injury.

About a year later, I began to experience some problems with my vision. After the constant issues with my eyesight I visited the doctor to have an eye exam. I was certain that I probably needed glasses. Throughout my career I have spent a lot of time in my vehicle. I've driven up and down the east coast from New York to Maryland to Florida. When I was booked on the west coast I would hop on a plane to cut down on time; but if the show was only a few hours away, I would hop in my car and take the road trip. I loved to drive.

During a few late nights on the road my vision was becoming pretty bothersome. I figured that my eyes were becoming fatigue. It was getting harder to read signs and traffic signals. I immediately scheduled an eye exam expecting to be told that I needed glasses for driving. During the examination, the doctor informed me that she needed to refer me to see a specialist. There was something going on with my eyes and her office was untrained to handle the issue. She insisted that I go immediately. A few days later I made my way to an eye doctor at the Washington Hospital Center. They did two hours of testing on my eyes. They tested me for a number of diseases and they were even considering some sort of cancer at one point. All of my tests came back negative. After more extensive testing it was determined that I had suffered a torn retina. The injury would require me to have surgery immediately to save my eyesight.

Having a torn retina was something I was unfamiliar with. The only time I've even heard of the injury was while watching a boxing match between Sugar Ray Leonard and Tommy Hearns. The fight was pretty brutal and Sugar Ray Leonard suffered a torn retina. He also needed to have surgery. The severity of the injuries was similar but my condition had become worse over time. The doctor told me that no matter what happened, I would never have good vision in that eye. My eye would never be normal again. I was told that the surgery was just to stop me from being totally blind. The doctor informed me that without the surgery, the eye would end up shriveling up and just being a dead eye. I couldn't take the chance of my eye dying, so I agreed to the procedure.

Before visiting the eye doctor, I was unaware of how serious my injury was. The doctors couldn't determine how long the retina had been torn, but all indications were that the injury was too far gone to repair. It is possible that another procedure could have been an option if the injury had been discovered earlier. But hearing the news in the Washington Hospital Center that day made me realize that I had to make a decision fast to make sure no further damage would be done. The surgery that followed was not to correct anything; it was too late for that. The surgery was done to save the eye.

The eye doctor scheduled my appointment right away. I went under the knife and prayed that everything would be successful. The doctors were spot on in their expectations of my vision. The surgery was a success and I made a full recovery but my eyesight never returned to normal. My eyes were not physically altered in any way. And for most people that see me, they can never tell that I underwent surgery. But as of today I am 90% blind in one eye. It is not the ideal situation considering what I do for a living.

I was also advised by the doctors to wear glasses. The glasses would not be used to help my vision. They informed me that I needed the glasses to protect my one good eye. My doctor reminded me that if I lose my good eye, I'm basically going to be a bona fide blind man. If I take my hand and put it over that good eye right now, I really can't see much. I would not be able to drive a car or do anything that required my full vision. I would basically be blind. For the past seven years that has been my struggle. I was told after the surgery that it would be a few months before I would notice a difference in my vision. They gave me a 50/50 chance that my vision would be fully restored after the surgery. Unfortunately my vision has only gotten worse.

I still remember the first night after I got out of the hospital. I was scheduled to do a show later that week and I refused to cancel. The comedy club that booked me did not want me to do the show; they wanted me to stay off the stage. I didn't listen. I still did the show. It was a local show that I thought it would be easy. I got on stage and the lights seemed to be coming at me. Everything was bright and overpowering. I really couldn't see anything. I had basically gone on stage forty-eight hours after having eye surgery. Performing that evening was extremely difficult. Even though it was hard for me to see, I managed to concentrate and walk my way through it. The audience never figured out that I couldn't see. They thought I was just joking about being blind in one eye.

About a week after my surgery I had to make a few adjustments to prepare myself to deal with my new reality. Being partially blind was something that I had to take serious. I never wanted my new condition to hinder me, so I tried to figure out ways to readjust my daily routine. I even made plans to make a fashion statement out of my new situation. I started looking on different websites for eye patches. I remember wanting to wear a fancy eye patch to match every outfit for my performances. I even wanted to get studs in my patch like Michael Jackson's glove. I had my mind made up that it was going to be awesome.

Even before my eye injury I added a Stevie Wonder joke into my show. That joke has been with me since the early 90s. I did that joke on *Showtime at the Apollo*, which was very dangerous at the time. Here I was, this unknown comedian, walking out on the Apollo stage, doing a Stevie Wonder joke on a stage that Stevie Wonder owns. It was very risky to do that. But it went over well, and the audience loved the joke. I still perform that joke in my comedy set to this day. The joke goes with my juggling bit when I compare myself to Stevie Wonder and Ray Charles juggling a few items. I drop the items in the middle of the bit and of course the audience eats it up. Ironically, now with my eye issue, that bit is hitting really close to home. Now it is almost a reality. If I lose the vision in my good eye, I am basically going to be legally blind.

Having one good eye is something that I rarely discuss in public. I never talk about it on stage. I've thought about writing a joke surrounding my vision and putting it into my act to bring attention to it. But I think even the people in my family don't know how humbling this is. It's a very serious wakeup call. I live with this every day knowing that I am 90% blind in one eye and dealing with the fear of protecting my good eye from any sort of injury. Everything relies on my good eye. I can't do what I do as a prop comic if I become blind. It's a very scary situation to be in. I try to forget about it as I go about my day, but most times it is always in the back of my mind.

I don't make a big deal about it when I'm working. Most people don't even know how serious it is. During my interviews I sometimes want to bring it up, but I never do. I have never informed my fans of my vision issue. It's non-existent as far as they know. This is my first public acknowledgement of my partial blindness. My family is aware that I went under the knife, but they never really followed up after the surgery to find out how my eye turned out.

I am a half-blind magician/comedian. I juggle knives, bowling balls and other strange items for a living. I do magic. I eat fire. I escape from straightjackets. That's how people know me. I do some stuff on stage that should require pretty good eyesight, but I've managed to do it with one eye, and I do it well. I still have a career even though I'm doing some very dangerous things with one eye. The next time you see me juggling a giant meat cleaver or a twelve-pound bowling ball, just remember that I'm doing it all with one good eye.

Epilogue

Throughout my journey I have been blessed to perform for millions of people across the world. I have showcased my talents on the smallest stages and worked my way to the bright lights of network television. From the first day I fell in love with magic I never looked back. I knew that I was going to be successful at all costs. I was going to do everything I could to make it in this business. If I was going to go down, I was going to go down in flames with a deck of cards in my hands. To make it to the biggest stages of the world is nothing short of a blessing. Every day I am grateful for my gifts.

There are no words to describe the feeling of watching a childhood dream come to life. When I gaze out into the sea of smiling faces as they enjoy my comedy set, I can't help but think of how my career has evolved. From the diverse crowds to the overseas gigs, the goal to showcase my love for magic and comedy has been realized. As my career continues to power forward, I know that there is much more work to do. I am excited for what the future holds.

People ask me all the time if I still get nervous when I perform. They are surprised when I tell them that I only get nervous when I perform in front of my family. No matter how many big stages I have conquered, I could never get rid of the butterflies I get when I know that my family is in the audience. Over the years I have created an on-stage persona that dazzles the audience. The *Kevin Lee* I transform

241

into on stage is confident, dominant and commanding. But in real life I am very different. When my family comes out to enjoy my shows, I am always reminded as to why I started this journey. Every gig that I have booked and every joke I have written has always been for my family. For the longest time, I convinced myself that I was letting my family down. I always wanted to reach the mega-movie-star heights and earn millions of dollars so that my family would never want for money again. I thought my family was disappointed in me. I could only imagine how they felt seeing other comedians in big budget films and television sitcoms. For many years I became self-conscious about not becoming a big star. I always wanted to be a huge success for them. Later in my career I had to realize that my family has and will always be proud of me. They have recognized my hard work over the years and have supported me throughout my crazy ride. Despite the nervousness that I feel when they watch me perform, it is always a good feeling to know that my family continues to root for me.

The entertainment industry is no easy puzzle to solve. There are many pitfalls and trapdoors that will stifle any performer if they are not careful. Millions of people have been chewed up and spit out by the business. Trying to be successful in the world of show business will not only change you, but it will also expose you. The industry has a way of magnifying your weaknesses. People often wonder why the gossip blogs and news segments are filled with countless performers that battle with drug addiction, depression, sex issues and out of control behavior. Many people fold under the hot light that the industry shines on them. The quest for money and fame will often bring the worse part of a person to the surface. However, the business will also help to bring out the best in people as well. For those headstrong entertainers, the industry can be a great vehicle to bring art and creativity to the world. I have survived many dark periods in my life by simply going on stage and binging laughter to an audience. Just weeks after my sister Dawn was murdered, I performed at a comedy club. Those forty minutes on stage helped to heal the pain stemming from our family tragedy—even if it was only for a few minutes.

I have been approached dozens of times by people who told me that they had been touched deeply by my act. One evening I met a fan who had recently lost a dear friend to cancer. He thanked me for making him laugh and helping him feel better about life. A similar incident happened with a young woman who recently lost her mother. She told me that her friends invited her out to see me and that it was the best decision she'd made to help ease her pain.

Bringing smiles to a large audience is the best feeling I could ever ask for. There is a shortage of moral victories in this business. The industry is filled with scores of dark days. But hearing the roar of laughter from a packed house makes up for all the hard work and stress of the business. I can't thank my family and fans enough for helping to keep my fire burning.

PLAYING WITH
FIRE

WWW.NEXTLEVELPUBLISHING.COM

Made in the USA
Middletown, DE
01 October 2020

20901975R00139